To Brittanny,

Life is about
love and
change.
God bless you
on your journey
to both.
Thank you for
everything you
do for my
sons!

Love,
Angélique

CHANGE
The Human Dis-Ease

BY

ANGELIQUE SILBERMAN

AuthorHouse

AuthorHouse™
1663 Liberty Drive, Suite 200
Bloomington, IN 47403
www.authorhouse.com
Phone: 1-800-839-8640

First published by AuthorHouse 11/2/2007

ISBN: 978-1-4343-4396-3 (e)
ISBN: 978-1-4343-4395-6 (sc)

Library of Congress Control Number: 2007907718

Printed in the United States of America
Bloomington, Indiana

This book is printed on acid-free paper.

Dedicated to

My sons, Timothy and Elijah, for seeing
me through life.
You have given me meaning beyond
anything else.

My father, Julian and mother, Julia, who
I know are with me every day.
My two sisters, Suzette Ann Sasha, and
Colette Lee who in their individual ways
have inspired me to change.

All people who want a better world.

THE HUMAN DIS-EASE

THE *Human Dis-ease* is the current state and disorder of a race of beings inhabiting this Earth right now who are powerless to make a lasting change in anything they touch. It is the *dis-ease* of our souls when we face challenges that should be easy, and the chaos that should be the natural order of creation, and manipulate them as human dramas that keep us all locked into a cycle of destruction. *Change occurs when we integrate a new concept into the order that we have already established. The dis-eased human psyche prevents us from making lasting changes. Perfect order and balance need to be established, which we cannot fulfill without love and compassion and the perfect understanding to permit those around us to follow their lives as they must.*

AUTHOR'S NOTE

WHY WOULD WE HAVE SCIENTIFIC PRINCIPLES, MATHEMATICS, AND UNIVERSAL LAWS REGARDING CHANGE THEORIES IN OUR WORLD IF WE CAN'T DO IT IN REAL LIFE? WE CAN TALK ABOUT IT AND EMBRACE IT, BUT NOTHING SEEMS TO STICK. IS THERE ANOTHER WAY THAT WE AREN'T LOOKING AT?

THIS hasn't been an easy book to write. It's mostly personal experience of a combined series of thoughts, impressions, years of human observation, and extensive reading. Like most people, I have been influenced by ancient and modern theories, some of which I discuss in an integrated way. Covering a vast compendium of information for the purposes of defining a new theory has its challenges. I would have loved to cover every topic I glance over, to highlight contradictions in our behavior in greater detail. I think that if you are interested in researching everything I embrace, references in the body of text should be a good starting point. I have endeavored to challenge you. Also, my writing style may be a little different than what you are used to. I do, in some instances, cover very sensitive topics, and I trust that you will humor me in my explanations throughout the book to explain each aspect in different ways. This is because I hope to show you that we are all capable of greatness and failure, as our history suggests. It was not my intention to make this an easy read. In the way I have presented my observations to you, I hope that you enjoy the processes and emotions you may feel while reading.

Angelique Silberman

For whom the bell tolls

No man is an island,
Entire of itself.
Each is a piece of the continent,
A part of the main.
If a clod be washed away by the sea,
Europe is the less.
As well as if a promontory were.
As well as if a manner of thine own
Or of thine friend's were.
Each man's death diminishes me,
For I am involved in mankind.
Therefore, send not to know
For whom the bell tolls,

It tolls for thee.

John Donne—Meditation XVII

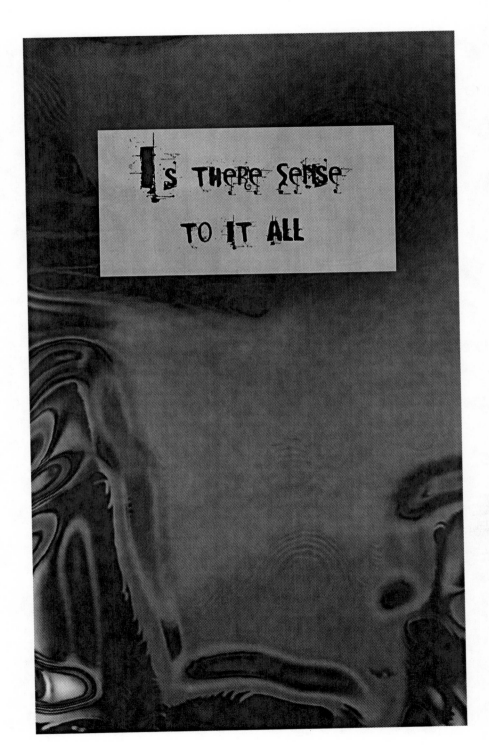

Is there sense
to it all

LIFE is hard. We live it, we deal with it, and we try to cope. What is the confusing chaos that we have classified as change? How do you manage to work the concept of change into your life, when all it resembles is turmoil, chaos, and confusion? You try to achieve and maintain balance when everything you hold dear is upside down. How do we as human beings stay in a state of balance emotionally, physically, sexually, and spiritually, when it seems to us as though the only time we can find some sort of equilibrium is to spiral out of control and find support from an outside source?

We have been led to believe that the only time we really find equilibrium is when we meditate, pray, or sequester ourselves away from the world and everything that resembles humanity in all its failing forms. Even though we are made out of matter found on this planet, even though we are living and breathing on this planet, we are all told that we need to live "outside" our reality in order to stay balanced and grounded. This is why we have collectively struggled to adjust to a changing world and have so many debilitating mental diseases today. We suffer from depression, anxiety, anguish, and lost hope, due to the fact that we have had to "split" our minds in two: what we want and what we think the world wants from us. It is as though most of us in the pursuit of happiness and balance started looking outside of ourselves and went on myth and vision quests to find answers. We have all sought the Holy Grail in some fashion, only to find that we have been led all the way back to the grandest mirror on the wall—reflecting back to ourselves the weaknesses and the strengths inherent within us. After all the heartache and disappointment of a cumulative effort of millions of years of research and theories, we are now being led to believe by our instincts that we are indeed defining our own reality. It is with our creative capacity that we, through the inner conflicts of thought and emotion, attract or repel the dynamic magnetic of our outer world. In so doing, we are able to project into the world whether we are attractive or repulsive, energetically speaking. We either attract or repel in a positive or negative fashion everything that we touch in the dimensional realities in which we find ourselves. Most of us are waking up to the realization that we can change our lives and live a balanced, harmonious existence without the search taking us to Tibet, monasteries, 400 hours of counseling, past-life regression, or tailor-made prayers. Being a seeker of knowledge and truth has its advantages, in that you can learn many things, but true change exists only in one area of your soul—that which is willing to sacrifice the way you have been doing things and integrate a whole new pattern into your life until it becomes you. We cannot just allow things to happen to us anymore without questioning why it is so. Why does it have to be like this or that? How do we stop other people's projection of their faults onto us and judge us by their yardstick and the ensuing abuse that follows?

The age of being politically correct has passed on to the era of finding your boundaries and setting a specific code of conduct in how you interact with reality and how it in turn treats you. These are all from the perspective that you can change other people's behavior towards you. You can demand more from your life when you start demanding more of yourself.

To top all of our paradigm shifts off, Mother Earth is waking up beneath us, in a raging fever, tossing off pollution and toxins buried within her skin. Half of what we have called a civilized world functions on the maiming and mistreatment of those that we deem disadvantaged, disempowered, or impoverished. Our "uncivilized" counterparts justify that they are trying to survive in a ruthless world that has always been so. Underdeveloped nations are only that way in that they have not developed their human and civil code of ethics in pace with their need for economic growth. The so-called "poor nations" are poor in one respect only: their inability to view a single human life as the most precious commodity. In these nations, mottos and creeds will usually encompass the discrediting statement "where one can be sacrificed for the many." We need to change this thinking, because it is always the one that leads the many, and what the hell are we going to do if we keep killing the "one" off? This imbalance is counter-weighted with the so-called "developed countries" in the world that are at war with one another for religious, political, economic, social, and moral reasons. Half of Africa's population is dying and leaving a fractured generation behind to cope with the little scraps that are left. We ignore all of this. We like to forget that there is a world out there, because *we are overloaded*—overloaded by basic truths that govern the great *universe of the unknown*. We are carrying a truckload of unknowns around with us that are Band-Aided together, in the hope that the whole load doesn't fall apart as we take another sharp corner. We overload our minds on a daily basis with things that may or may not happen, and worry about the things in life we cannot change, and yet feel powerless to change the things we can.

What is the answer?

Taking accountability and stepping into the unknown of your psyche is a frightening notion. We distract ourselves with anything we can, so that we don't have to face who we actually are. I've actually heard someone say that every time they try to change or improve themselves in any way, bad things happen to them, so they can't disturb the status quo. The psyche was the Greek concept of the self, encompassing the modern ideas of soul, self, and mind. The Greeks believed that the soul or "psyche" was responsible for behavior. Carl Jung, lifelong student of the unconscious mind, did not differ in his opinions.

Who are you really? How do you define yourself against the outside world? Is it with your weight, your eating habits, your victimizations, your addictions, your looks, your age, your height? How do you respond when people ask: *Who are you? What are you?*

Do you answer with what you do for a living, as a means to define yourself in a group of people? Being an accountant, say, would define you immediately as someone intelligent enough to stick your hand in the matrix of digits and come out with a workable solution. You are immediately classified as dependable, solid, and secure, and probably even a suitable mate. Whereas being a deejay in a traveling show might have the opposite reaction. Do you answer with your birth name, gender, race, religion, or any of the other labels you have been branded with in this life by the people around you—or worse, yourself? Financial institutions are the keeper of these questions that can only be answered by the human credit rating: whether you are a good or a bad person; stable, sensible, and mature, or a hustler in the game of life, a "gangsta" on the streets. Is there no other option between the light you live in and the darkness you have labeled as *weird* or *out there*—the place you dare not venture into without the help of a gun filled with ammunition called judgments?

You are armed and ready to face the unknown, like a commander facing his troops, and you may as well come out and say, "We are going in hot. Locked and loaded, armed to the teeth, troops. This is not a job for the weak and weary, so if any of you are afraid, I suggest you stay behind. If you see anything move in the dark or the forest of the unknown you don't recognize, kill it."

So out you go into the world, armed with 5,000 years of programming, and dangerous to the extent that you have all judgments of yourself and the world at your disposal, and are prepared to use them at will. Sometimes—in fact most of the time—you have the judgment gun aimed right at your own temple, in the fear that you are facing enemy territory and are terrified of making a mistake. So you start at the beginning of your life, making judgments all over the place—being the academic, the class clown, the rebel, the bully, the victim, or the Casanova at school. You attack and rebel, simultaneously, in an effort to make sense of the world around you, but you are attacking your way out of one bunker and into the next battlefield of your teens, where your enemy now becomes the emotions. Some of us rebel against our very natures, sometimes actually going so far as to totally ignore parts of ourselves, like our spirituality, sexuality, vibrancy, bodies, and everything that resembles something out of the ordinary or uncontrollable. The very first thing we seek in our world is control. The last of which—

ourselves—lays suffering in the tethers of bondage, seeping out life in every instance of controlled behavioral modifications we have imposed. We can't take the time to understand the motivations of why people do things. Just because we don't know about it doesn't mean it didn't happen. We can, at best, tolerate the differences we have, and when we can't, we are faced with the biggest killer of the soul and imagination: indifference. This is the point we reach when the gap in differences becomes so wide and the bridge too expensive to build. We turn our backs in frustration at not being able to exercise our will on the lives of others, and we write them off.

Oh, shock! We are so taken by surprise when faced with change. When everything we are structured around is about maintaining the infrastructure of our personal belief systems or what we believe ourselves to be. Ignorantly, we believe our personalities to be absolute and beyond the limitations of being able to change.

The human existence is centered on the eventuality of love and the happy ending, not knowing or being willing to accept that it is really up to us to make those endings in every chapter of our lives. The process, no matter how you shuffle the cards, ends up with one major turning point: change. Change, or chaos, is part of a universal law carefully designed to be the beginning of dynamic learning and growth. Without it, nothing would exist. Yes, my friend, it is you, and the change you accept or reject, that will shape your life and the destiny that you so gladly seek. It is you and only you that will find the keys to your own salvation and the passage out of the personal hell you are going through right now. No one can hand them to you, because your key is like no one else's. There is only one and that one is *you*.

CHANGE AS
A CONDITION

CHAOS theory has been loosely defined from a few schools of thought, in that particular systems that the theory describes are apparently disordered. However, chaos theory is really about finding the underlying order in seemingly random data and information. It is from a collection of thoughts that *The Butterfly Effect* hypothesis was described as:

"The flapping of a single butterfly's wing today produces a tiny change in the state of the atmosphere. Over a period of time, what the atmosphere actually does diverges from what it would have done. So, in a month's time, a tornado that would have devastated the Indonesian coast doesn't happen. Or maybe one that wasn't going to happen, does." (Ian Stewart, *Does God Play Dice? The Mathematics of Chaos*)

Changing your world is not as difficult as it looks from where you are sitting. It may seem impossible to grasp this concept of change and how to ride the horse as it gallops with you, at full tilt, on its back. Change is a volatile substance and like mercury, looks different in every light and circumstance that it interacts with. It is, however, the one thing that we as humans are created to manifest in our lives while we are here: the epic struggle of balancing the willingness for stability and with the constant flux of reality. There are so many experiences occurring, so many things happening without our involvement and without our permission, that the human psyche tries to create order from the perpetual chaos that surrounds it. Therefore, we set up a string of actions and reactions that allows us to accept change conditionally. Much has been said about semantics and belief change systems, but actualizing this process as common practice is still in its human infancy stage. We can, on condition, accept a changing environment. Our judgments are placed in denial for a time until we get used to a changing environment or until we deem ourselves "ready" to face the situation. We are, in the interim, paralyzed with fear of what will happen next and how that in turn will affect the entire dynamical processes that stem from where we are in life. We also accept change in others and write a set of prescribed processes to follow—sometimes without discussion with the other party.

"You can love me on this condition."

"You have hurt me, so in order to get back to where we were, you have to follow these conditional rules."

"So-and-so is not following this-and-that path, so we will impose these conditions on them until they 'see the light.'"

These are some of the governing opinions that we blindly impose on other people in order to make sense of the internal chaos we feel when things are starting to veer out of our control. What is even more interesting is that all of these thoughts occur outside of behavior and in the inner workings of the mind. This is entirely self-motivated, in an effort to gain control over one's set of circumstances and the ideals of a perfect existence. We are all honestly striving for perfection, but in this world, with the laws of science, astronomy, and mathematics governing order in our part of the universe, commonalities lie with one theory that we don't buy into—chaos is creation in motion.

So here we are. At this point in our evolution, we are looking at change and how we cope with the strange psychological makeup of not wanting or needing change, but at the same time craving something to happen to us, something out of the ordinary, and it better be something bloody spectacular! We are all looking for the fireworks of love, the tranquility of peace, and the ability for the people we love to accept us unconditionally and not try to change or control us. To admit that we are indeed dull and bored with ourselves, with our society, and with one another is ludicrous. We are all so happy with who we are and what we do that we never try to re-invent our wheels by buying new clothes, new cars, change our hairstyles or change partners. We try superficially to change but the underlying pattern is still the same and the outcomes are unchanged. We never wish for happy-ever-after outcomes and we never covet different lives. The very thing we crave is the very thing we do not accept into our reality. We have come to the common perception that change is something that "happens" to us. Poof! Out of the blue. Like an accident, an illness, a life-threatening event, or a fleeting moment that sparks our interest in a television show. We never want or welcome change; we always accept it as part of our world—something that happens.

Scientists have proven that changes occur in the spaces between molecules, atoms, and cells, as well as within the cells themselves. In computer database terminology, an *atomic change* is an indivisible change—it can succeed entirely or it can fail entirely, but it cannot partially succeed.

For the last 5,000 years, since the early beginnings of formalized modern religion, we have, as mankind, begun to look at the physical or cellular structure of our environment and surrounding worldscape. The times are changing, and many of those on the planet at this time have known, or are beginning to know, that something is different about our world and the way we are moving within it. There are thousands of accounts of animal behavioral changes, like a cheetah nursing the baby of a baboon she just killed, or sharks stalking particular swimmers. We, on the other hand, superimpose the immediate; NOW, NOW, NOW! If it can't be downloaded into our heads in fifteen minutes or delivered in a compact, concise manner that only we understand, it is labeled "*junk: having a superficial appeal or utility, but lacking substance*" and discarded for someone else to recycle.

We huddle in groups and discussion boards and discuss why that is so, but the conclusions are vague and mystical, even though there are times when we can provide the much-needed human proof by underscoring theories with scientific, archaeological and medical fact. We think that it is on an individual scale because that is how we have been conditioned to think. Insular. Isolated. Private and confidential.

Little do we actually understand that our spiritual searches for truth, relationship problems, changing family dynamics, changing identities, and ambiguous sexual orientation are human themes we all have in common. We all prefer to think that our problems are insulated, that our struggles are all our own.

Look at the breakdown on a practically epidemic scale in the last fifty years in male-female relationships and the structure of the institution of marriage. What the hell is going on? Scientists, mystics, and prophets all have theories. We are seeing traditional roles reformatted like a hard drive in a computer, only to have us all start all over again. We are steeped in a deep frustration, and frustration is the killer of creativity and growth of soul. What was masculine is now bordering on feminine, and vice- versa, and we are left staring blankly into one another's eyes, wondering where the hell to go next.

We also need to look at the social environment to see those stereotypical judgments in effect in the milieu in which we interact. Men are taking on the more submissive roles in society as the homemaker, as opposed archaically to the hunter and gatherer. I recall fondly the fairy tales of my youth, where the prince rescued the princess from a life with dwarves, death by magic, and younger women who married the rich and powerful king. Everyone who was good was handsome or beautiful, and everyone in these stories who lived on the dark side was evil in intent and ugly. Damn! Hard line for men to live up to. It is not just men and women as defined classes for we have an ever increasing number of people who are embracing non-specific gender types and roles. The rest of us are confused enough about where we are, let alone having to contend with an alternate lifestyle. Not even the fairy tales or fables could help us in our predicament. It is even more disconcerting when we should be looking at our own struggles and finding a better way to do things, instead of hating and condemning other choices. Most of us have a library of books that we fumble through, tear a few pages out of context, and hurl them at people who defy the normality rule.

So, here we are, a generation of women, poisoned by apples of temptation, threatened by ostracism, and frightened into secluded towers, waiting to be rescued from the acronyms of the CEO driving the BMW, and yes, wait for this—to live happily ever after.

Ladies and gentlemen, we have bred in front of us a generation of unrealistic expectations placed on the men, while we disempower the women. Clever plot. What we tell our children has been passed, without scrutiny, from generation to generation, and this is what keeps the next generation bound, much like the old biblical saying "the sins of the father will be passed on to the sons."

We have all the information in front of us. We have and always will see everything in life from our own point of view!

I think that we use biblical references to quiet a yearning soul, most of the time taking things out of context and juxtaposing them next to our conscience to ease transitions between our reality and who we aspire to be. This is the silent communism we have bought into. The cliché "everything happens for a reason" is a popular one and is used to cover a field full of weeds like a generic poison. This phrase dulls the screaming emotions of questioning why and how, and squashes the terror and rage of feeling powerless against the full force of life. When we allow ourselves to feel that deeply and trigger the fear again, we are adept at verbalizing the famous "life happens" or "life is hard." Have you really allowed yourself to feel anything before justifying the emotion with a cliché? In my observation, the greater the use of clichés, the greater the amount of emotional denial in the presence of fear, especially when used in the context of *"what will be will be."* I have known no greater movement away from personal accountability than a title from a song. It is denial of self in its most palpable form. This is like wielding your "judgment gun" in a forest in the middle of the night, pretending not to be afraid and therefore avoiding emotional so-called weakness and yelling, "If I am meant to die, then I am ready."

No one knows where this ignorance came from and no one really cares until someone gets hurt. Are we hurting yet? Do we feel pain?

We have now become a generation of dead people, dead to our own feelings. We revere love, joy, and happiness, and then we run as fast as our little legs can carry us from pain, fear, and anger like the plagues of the past. We huddle from night sweats and haunting nightmares. We see most of our feelings as weaknesses and hide the part of us that feels that way on a daily basis, labeled in the dark as "bad," and then we run like hell into what light we have left and into the arms of people who reflect that love back to us. What has happened when we have finally found out that those arms of love were as empty as our own? There is a brief moment of introspection and blame-placing; either on ourselves or on the other now-guilty party, and we are off and running on that vicious cycle of finding the ultimate happiness. Some of us manage to hide this better than others behind criticisms and judgments while others get labeled more. Therein lies the crux.

The Latin word *crux* defines simply: *cross*. The cross forms an intersection of two forms, planes, ideas, or points of origin. So let's presume for a minute that we are moving along our life in a straight line from A to B as it were, life to death, when we come across a period in our lives that collides at the intersection of thoughts, ideas, or decisions that allow us to rise into higher thought or effect a spiritual quantum leap.

One of my favorite books (*The Isaiah Effect—Decoding the Lost Science of Prayer and Prophesy by Gregg Braden*) outlines a road in making different choices with our lives that enable us to reach into higher planes of existence than we think we are capable of.

At our life's crosses or intersections, we are at a space where change has succeeded in getting us to catch up, and we are asked to look at ourselves honestly. What happens at this point is so individual that nobody can help us, no matter how we run to others for solace, guidance, or direction. Which way do I go? What is the outcome down each path? Which is the right decision? It is in this process that you should get to know yourself enough to make a decision based on how you feel about each path. How often do you tell yourself that you are going to make a choice about what feels right to you and not what seems right to your family, friends, or co-workers? Most of us lack that integrity and faith in self and the absolute accountability for who we are and our position in our world. Moreover, we are during a change process more afraid of death than fear, and we would rather go with the flow than try to stand up and say "this is who I am and this is what I choose." In the crux, you stand accountable, and if you can stay centered in it for long enough, you may actually learn something about yourself; it may surprise you as to the greatness you can achieve through your own quantum leap.

FEAR KNOCKED AT THE DOOR.

FAITH ANSWERED.

AND, LO, NO ONE WAS THERE

- AUTHOR UNKNOWN

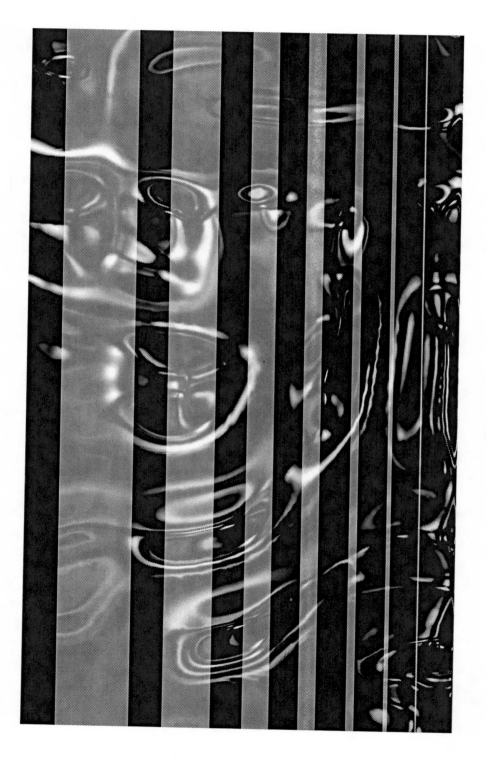

PARADIGM SHIFTING AND THE ART OF NORMALITY

WE are hurting in the human race. We are thinking in the molecular structure which is stationary and insulated—just individuals locked up within their pain, all alone. It is as though we have been conditioned by an invisible entity to believe that as humans, we are not capable, competent, or useful. We think that because we can see no tangible signs of life in our immediate galaxy, we are all alone. Isolation breeds its own insecurity. We have blamed ourselves in the worst way by blaming our egos for getting in the way of our growth. Sigmund Freud dedicated most of his life to the understanding and definitions of ego. Although much of his work was groundbreaking and has become a modern standard of reference and contention, I find the following insight most interesting:

"The ego is not sharply separated from the id; its lower portion merges into it .... But the repressed merges into the id as well, and is merely a part of it. The repressed is only cut off sharply from the ego by the resistances of repression; it can communicate with the ego through the id." (Freud's 1923 paper, "The Ego and the Id")

Our egos have been downgraded in status only so that we can compare ourselves to one another in order to see our personal worth. We have read books and educated ourselves to elevate our egos into a higher status than what they have deserved, and constantly strived for perfection through comparisons. Is it really that piece of paper that makes you a better person, or is it a badge that you have labeled yourself with to define your personality? It may make you more qualified in the current socioeconomic competitiveness and may allow you more financial benefits, but how are you functioning in your heart? I have met so many professionals who wanted to be firemen, artists, or professional nomads. These yearnings are filed as childhood dreaming. The passion that created those dreams is left in a box in the "denial cage" in the mind. We like to stereotypically joke about the passionless professions, but we have to start looking at the buried passion and true courage inside the human to understand what it must have taken to sell your dreams out in order to survive in this world. It is the rare few truly mad and ideological who follow their hearts in the great unknown of this world, who charter new territory that will become landmarks—good or evil—for the world to integrate into future processing.

It is only with the help of our higher ideology and the eventual total acceptance of self that we can look into the mirror and appreciate everything that went into our creation and continues to grow within us. Instead, we idolize other humans, separating them by status, image, and the aging human form, all the while comparing ourselves to supermodels, movie stars and rock stars all over the world. We need to compare ourselves to something other than what we perceive as ordinary, run-of-the-mill, or passé. So we perpetuate our idols by buying their goods, watching the fruits of their labor, and modeling ourselves after them. We don't really want to be who we really are. There is plenty of modern technology to help us re-sculpt, reshape, and reform ourselves into anything we want to be in the effort to "be the best we can be."

This is "superficial renovating." We all lack the ability for the massive task of internal restructuring when most of us look at life in a purely physical manner, demanding more attention and energy from others than they are really capable of giving. We accuse others of stealing our energy and not being able to be around negative people. Yet that is the very thing we are trying to avoid looking at within ourselves. I have met some of the most negative, self-effacing people, and watched as they removed themselves from social groups or assigned blame on "negativity around them."

We blame those who birthed us and raised us, accusing them often publicly of the fallibility of being human, which we feel absolves us from any true responsibility. We idolize mentors and the gods of our time, and arrange a suitably public lynching when they fall short of our idealism. We all have, within our darkest selves, the capability to become thieves, murderers, rapists, and child molesters, because we were raised by a misunderstanding, drunken, or abusive hand, in turn making our victims feel the pain that we felt as an innocent child. We can make use of lover after lover, ignoring their feelings or the capability to be hurt because we in turn are broken and bruised. We tell ourselves that we are not "ready" for commitment and may even be as honest as to share that with others who love us, all the while knowing that the other has more caring and devotion toward the time spent together. We feign attention and affection to get what we want. It doesn't matter what we want at the time, as long as we get it. We might even go so far in our dishonesty, especially when there is a lot to lose, as to fake love.

It is interesting to watch the human choice; it will not choose a job or person that embodies passion because it is deemed childish, irresponsible, and irrational. Yet the mind of the child exists in day-to-day interaction with the outside world, manipulating and contorting reality until it is more acceptable. The cycle of taking responsibility for the feelings we have has to start somewhere, and making someone else bear the responsibility and suffering for the pain and hurt we feel is not only irresponsible, but it is the pure definition of evil.

Everybody loves the feeling of being able to be a social chameleon and just "fit in," but we can't because we are currently going through life looking from the outside in, not from the inside out. It doesn't work anymore. This is why most people are feeling alienated and alone, seeking places of refuge and solace in hobbies and interests that are more individual. Coupledom is at its most climactic point, with partners choosing to "go it alone" more than they do in trying to work things out. We share the common feeling that we deserve more and better than what we already have. This is a universal sign that something is deeply wrong and we are still looking outside the window at society, the Internet, our cell phones, religion, our families, and money as the root cause of evil. Why can't we finally look within to see the cause of evil within our psyches and the master of these—guilt and denial of self?

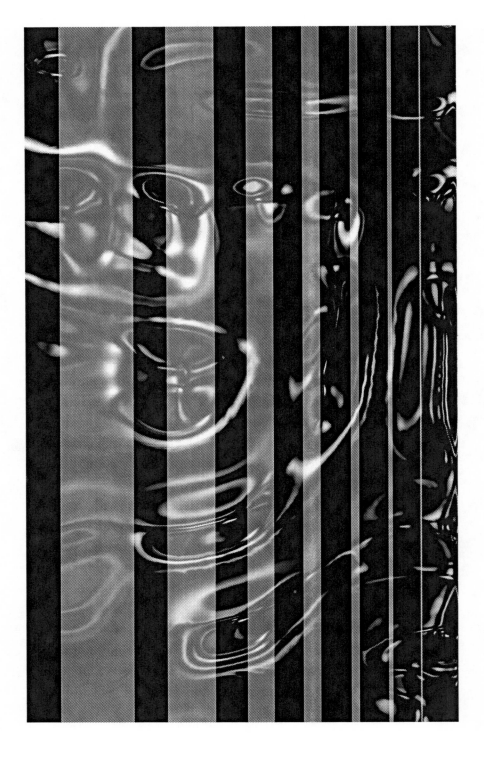

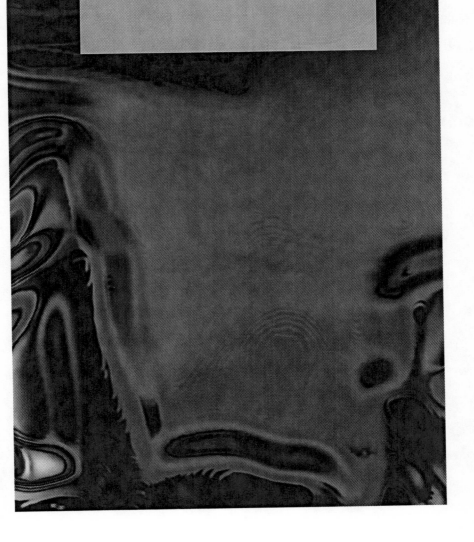

THE WHITE ARMY

MOST of us have seen a red blood cell at one time or another in our lives. Vibrant healthy little trampolines of regeneration, flipping back and forth a zillion times in their life cycle between the heart and the lungs and the rest of our vast mostly oxygen-starved body. Within the human body, about 3 billion living cells die every minute. White blood cells live for about thirteen days. Red blood cells die every 120 days, while the liver cells can live for up to 100 years, if they don't have to contend with excessive processing. All these little cells bombing back and forth, back and forth, tirelessly programmed for life. Every red blood cell is vibrant and healthy and seemingly independent of one another, but unified in purpose, and this purpose is to support life, to support us. Just another day at the office until something interesting happens—there is a change, a metamorphosis. A quantum leap in that one cell somewhere in the body snaps and mutates into a renegade. This free radical could remain healthy and do what everyone else is doing, but becomes the antagonist in this wonderful "Eden" of life support. Bing-badda-boom! This cell mutates spontaneously into something else, a dis-ease from the old French word *desaise* or *"lack of ease."* A faulty functioning of a system or process which leads us to be at odds with what the rest of the clan is doing. Suddenly the alarms go off. There are no buzzers alerting the white-cell troops to what is happening. The rest of the body just knows that there is going to be fireworks.

It's as though the mass consciousness of the physical signals a red alert and goes on a defense that starts the chain reaction. The body goes to war and engages in battle. Some days are better than others, and victories are made for the good guys, while other days there are huge losses and the bad guys get to gain ground on the destruction. Our logical mind and spirit are unaware of this, but our subconscious puts out the all-points bulletin. We either do something about this or

27

we ignore it. Maybe subconsciously inside us—the place where no one really wants to look—is a place where we just want everything to run its course. We tend to accept this at a deep level as *the way things should be or are*" or that *"this kind of thing runs in the family,"* and all this happens because secretly we have been harboring a fatalistic viewpoint on our life that nothing good can come of anything here anyway. Behind every mortal or transformational death we experience is the absolute so-called reality that everything is accepted to have its own time and place, and sooner or later, everything comes to an end.

Where did we get this notion, and has anybody managed to question why we think that everything alive or inanimate must come to the inevitable conclusion? Why is death such an absolute conclusion? We use this worn-out excuse to compromise relationships, make sense of feelings that just aren't there anymore, and pretend that there is no explanation to life hereafter. So we have come to the human conclusion that dead is dead after all, and there is nothing anyone can say about it without being labeled as a lunatic or flake. How would we cope if we actually thought in real time that there is no death? Maybe this whole "sustaining life" thing is too tiring or we have forgotten how to make sense of all the bullshit anyway. Some of us fight, maybe our partners fight for us, and through that show us something we never saw in ourselves before. Maybe we find a higher purpose to the dis-ease and show others how to cope with theirs, and maybe our own cause-and-effect has led us to this point to be put in someone else's shoes. In any case, due to the nature of our world as we have created it, we stumble forward, looking beyond the white cells that are fighting for our lives, to the men and women in white coats for the cure. We are poked and prodded, and our healers give us the final verdict—that of a degenerating dis-ease. All hell breaks loose. Some little rogue cell has enabled our entire body to form a coalition and together, fight an invader. This little mutation has now caused us as individuals to panic. Our ego goes into self-preservation mode. Panic leads to fear. Fear makes us lose control, and that loss of control puts us in a depressed emotional state. Now, not only are we suffering under the dictatorship of dis-ease, but we are depressed too! Sure, some of us fight, but now there is the never-ending quieting of our passion for life, the melancholy self-pitying depression that becomes the biggest battle. More often than not, this is when God hears from us—whichever God we believe in. Our first conversation with God may even start like this:

"Why now?"

We may even graduate to the blame stage, to this God we haven't spoken to in so long, and even though He or She may have been waiting eighty years to talk to you, you have this to say:

"How could you let this happen to me?"

"I hate you."

So, if we follow the progression of this cell, what was once a biological, purely physical change has become a mental and finally, the inevitable, spiritual battle, which is usually heralded by the "why me" statement. Why can't we look at this battle as an opportunity to look at the melancholia that led us to this point? Perhaps if you believe that your soul is older than this generation, you may be able to trace back feelings of being ineffective to the very beginning of time. We are all walking around with the proverbial monkey on our back that chatters in our mind constantly, asking us the five points of marketing: who, when, where, why, and what is everything all for?

Our question in the beginning of time was "who created the light and dark," which led us on a quest for God and our personal aspiration to create our own light to equal our perception. We sought to bring our own light on Earth, which heralded the birth of fire. Is the natural conclusion at this point in our disillusioned evolution that everything created in our world is there for one purpose only, to teach us as spiritual beings? Most of this entire trend is toward the feeling that life is not about the "we," so much as it is about "me." We are obviously not alone, and by looking at the battles of the sick and diseased, we see the clear indication of how it is when we are changing or mutating. We reach out to others and now, more importantly, we reach into ourselves. Like an ever-expanding spiral in both directions reaching for greater purpose, meaning, and growth, we expand through change. Some of us reach out to God—or by whatever name you may call the Creator—and find solace and answers in the prayers or intentions of your faith. Others have lost faith in hope for our lives, our religions, and in humanity in general. This is a dangerous time in history, when we are a humanity of faithless, unfocused, and emotionless people. It is only natural that our deepest fears of change in this area are about to be challenged by mutating, and the only foreseeable way for this to occur is for us to remain so disconnected from source that we destroy that which gives us life, this planet. There is no other flexible conclusion in the equation to try to jerk us out of this robotic stance we have taken against ourselves and the world around us. There is no fear that the environmentalists can engender in us greater than the fear of us actually doing something about our apathetic behavior crystallized in the verbalization of "what's the use, anyway." No one thing can make another thing move unless it decides that inertia is a useless practice and decides to engage in change. We will categorically, uniformly, and coherently avoid changing ourselves, and continue to believe that death is the only path to changing anything, because after that, we don't care.

Who the hell are we kidding? We don't care anyway. We will consistently choose to nip death at the heels like a young bear, until it wakes up and opens its mouth. Then, like a terrified pup, we will run and try to find somewhere to hide. This time, we have exhausted all other hiding places and what we avoid facing the most will be our dogcatcher with a net we can't escape. This is the choice all of us make unconsciously every day, unified in our perceptions and slowly creating that which we fear the most. In the meantime, we place our faith in an abstract religion, modern medicine, and science and technology, while more of us place our faith in our family and friends, hoping that these things will prevent us from the harshness of what we now call reality.

"EVERY BODY PERSEVERES IN ITS STATE OF BEING AT REST OR OF MOVING UNIFORMLY STRAIGHT AHEAD, EXCEPT INSOFAR AS IT IS COMPELLED TO CHANGE ITS STATE BY FORCES IMPRESSED."

(FIRST LAW OF MOTION, SIR ISAAC NEWTON 1687
OF THE PRINCIPIA MATHMATICA
[COHEN & WHITMAN 1999 TRANSLATION]).

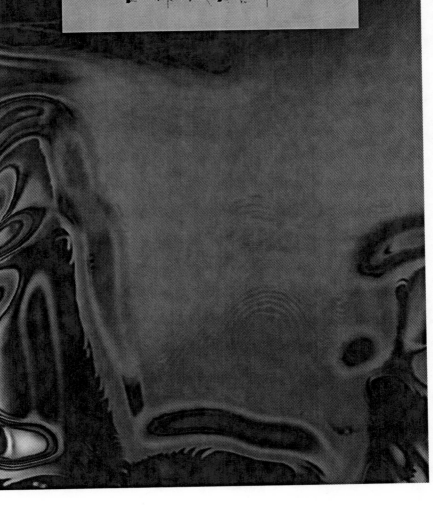

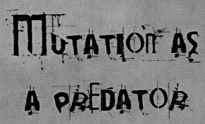

I HAVE read and heard the tales about warriors, lone revolutionaries, and I ponder that their solace must have come from deep inside themselves, in a place where I have never been; a marvel of the landscape of the soul, and perhaps someday maybe I will see it for myself. The place where everything you are makes sense and you can actually believe in everything you are. No matter how many times you are beaten down to change your mind, you always follow the indomitable path of self-knowledge. As a young girl, I formalized the idea that I wanted to be "normal." What made me think that I was abnormal in the first place is beyond me now. Maturity, being bashed by life has taught me that life imitates art and there is no normality here. I came into this world in the late sixties, when we were supposed to have moved into the Aquarian Age. My mother found that there was no free thinking in her society about a previously divorced, deserted, unwed mother giving birth to a daughter born in the *Year of the Fire Horse.* Thank God it was South Africa and not China a hundred years ago, for I would not be alive to tell the tale. Back then, female children were killed at birth, as they were considered difficult to marry off. In the nucleus of my family, the event caused quite the stir. Traditional Catholic upstanding parents—rogue daughter who has mutated—the family gathers around and wonders what to do with the dis-ease. The "Angels of Mercy," as I like to think, had a quick chat with my grandmother, who took me in and rescued me from the sea of adventures my mother would navigate, before I finally became part of a family. I realize that I am fortunate, for there are many people whose stories have touched my soul in this lifetime, but they have had to wage the battle with the demon of abandonment on their own. One day, if one of my cells goes ballistic, I won't be able to blame it on the other side of the family.

My DNA dad is alive and well; he just chose not to be a father. His choice. My choice was to get over it and come to completion as a human being, doing the same thing everybody else does: support life. At first, in my youthful exuberance, I overcompensated for this and tried to become everybody's buddy. My teenage friends would hang out and sip copious amounts of coffee and hot chocolate at my house when they had nothing "better" to do. My inadequacy had me by the short-and-curlies. I fetched and carried and I cried, but what I remember most about my childhood was too much responsibility for me to handle, and trying too damn hard to make it all fit. Not much changed; I just became a workaholic instead, trying to bury my face in the invisible, never-ending pile of work that manifested as fast as I needed it to. And when the pile finally started whittling away, I would immerse myself in a blinding workout schedule and fall hungry and exhausted into a fitful sleep.

The only thing I had to cling on to were the words of a man uttered to his adoring granddaughter, distorted through a child's perception: that the world was a special place and that I had my own special place in it. Good or bad, right or wrong, it was the guiding light of salvation for me, swimming in a sea of desperation, hoping that I was really going to die before I was thirty-three.

I was at this time motivated only by one thought: that we are all here at this time in the evolution and co-creation of the relative unknown and the beauty of creation. Peace and solace escaped me like a mercenary fighting a lost cause. Natural disasters and human failures passed like ghosts through my broken psyche, and I was driven forward in the faithlessness that indeed everybody and everything was happening for a reason, and that eventually I would build my own picket fence and find my personal "happily-ever-after."

We are all slowly starting to realize that, as an uncomfortable and uneasy human society, we are dis-eased. Our subconscious has been sending out the rap sheet for a while now, but we have been too busy with the distraction drama of our own humanity, which we have been experiencing with our five senses. Oh, have we been clever about creating and keeping the distraction alive! We hire scientists who reinforce the physical nature of our universe. We choose not to listen to the ones who differ from the common opinion, and we label them with distrust. We tell ourselves that if it were real, we would see it. We pacify our need for spirituality with clichés, much like feeding the dog scraps at the table. "Fido wants a bowl of food, but we toss him the bone sans any meat."

We have deified a whole system of carefully instructed medical teams that deny the very existence of a holistic approach to health, and paralyze the very nature of traditional healers who did the same service for thousands and thousands of years before Hippocrates was credited for a developing the Oath. We recount stories of the sick dying at the hands of a healer, and excuse facts that modern medicine has stacked up a higher toll of lives. People have died in hospitals, waiting for doctors to attend to them. These doctors are overworked, and hospitals are understaffed. Yet we label others as kooks and quacks. Our judgments of medicine have placed the emphasis on restorative health and not on prevention of disease. Our own care of the bodies we travel around this world in is in disarray, and we need only glance at the state of health care in every country in existence today to know. Cancer, previously reserved for the elderly and the unlucky, is now a very widespread disease, consuming young, fit, healthy, and dynamic people, as well as those further along in their prime. It's commonly referred to as one disease or a single condition, but it's actually a group of more than 100 different diseases. These diseases are characterized by uncontrolled growth and spread of abnormal cells, which divide in a haphazard manner. The end result is that they commonly pile up to form a non-structured mass or tumor.

We live in an era like none before. It is an age of chemically enhanced, genetically modified, and hormonally induced foods. Yet, the enchantment with perfection leads us to buy these processes and endorse them. The obvious lack of vitamins and minerals in our diets goes unheeded. It's too expensive or too vile for our tastes. Conventional medicine requires methodical metering so that we don't fall off the path of getting better. We must develop ways to remind us how to be healthy or how to stay fit.

We live in an age of open disclosure, where we all have access to information on products that we ingest, plaster on ourselves, or expose ourselves to. We are sandwiched between idioms of "it will never happen to me" and our machismos "I'm strong enough to handle it." If our body is the temple that our Creator intended it to be, then we are worshipping something most of us know nothing about. And we don't care.

WAR ON WORK

H

ISTORY and evolution have dictated our roles and what jobs we have been allowed access into for reasons as diverse as war, famine, industrialization, technology, and survival. Women have only really gained entrance into what has been deemed a "stable workforce" in the last hundred years, whereas men have traditionally been the "breadwinners," and based their self-esteem on being the primary provider, as opposed to the primary caregiver. Through trials and tribulations of being refused entry, discrimination, and plain ostracism— ethnic origins, cultural diversity, and sexual biases have made it very difficult to gain employment, let alone meaningful employment.

We have spiritually jailed ourselves in no more dramatic and undisclosed nature than in the way of we work and the resulting fruits thereof. We have willingly sold ourselves into slavery to our lifestyles, and place the best hours of the day and the best years of our lives into work, to sustain the very thing that we want and then never find the time to enjoy anyway. This not only epitomizes the workers of this world, but the many of us who remain addicted to substances and violence: The homeless who believe there is no other place for them than standing on a street, staring blankly at the glossy life that remains out of reach. The human warrior, armed with illegal weapons in modern battle armor, fighting for the rights of a street culture. This is a world where basic needs and opportunities are as limited as the life expectancy it dictates.

I truly believe that not only do we create our world, but also that our world mirrors what we do. Why are there so many people locked in jail, banned from living with the rest of us because they have become such a danger to themselves or society? Robbery, drugs, murder, and motive of the big payday will allow you to fast-track your life in a prescribed eternity from the rest of your peers, behind bars. These are forgotten souls, in that they are an embarrassment to their families. People want to forget crimes borne out of hate, and lock the perpetrator away to live out the rest of their days in a room no bigger than most bathrooms. Jails are a reflection of our society and how we worship money at the cost of everything else, even our own personal freedoms. Just about everybody "employed" in the modern machine works for compensation, and that compensation in our lifetime is the paper and metal currency that is tied to some sort of hard commodity, mostly gold, hidden deep in the folds of society. We are all prospectors in search of the vein of life—fool's gold—that will sustain our existence. We are capable of spilling the blood of another human being if it dares step in the path of the lust we embody. We will lie, cheat, beg, steal, and borrow from the world's banks to get what we want or where we think we should be because we in some way deserve it. Funny thing is that those who think they deserve something are never the ones who receive what they want. It is those who are at peace with the inner workings of themselves who become authentically empowered, and magnetically attract everything they desire in the perfect magic of manifestation.

Almost the entire known world works for money and the trade of goods for same. Seeing as though most everyone I know feels that money is dirty or a "necessary evil," it is hardly fitting to place one's time and energy into the acquisition of something evil and dirty, now is it? It is time we brought reason and understanding into this by looking at our assumptions as to why we do this to ourselves.

Since the gain of money is tied to expending of one's energy in some manner, we all have to put forth our talents and education in a way that is pleasing and good. We place our personality, history, talents, skills, and appearance on the line in order to compete in an ever-growing and expanding population. The lines between who we are and what we want to be are getting longer and longer and further apart.

In the same way that we expel disease in cells, we begin to get caught up in the lack of control that we have in our work environment, and that presents us with the new quandary of depression. It places us further from our goals to maintain the lifestyle, and closer to having to move in search of fulfillment and even worse, avoiding unemployment. For most of our egos, it is the yellow line of failure to engage, the retreat into alienation from the society we were striving to be part of in the first place. Welcome to the *bank of the streets,* a place where the gun is being used like a debit card, and human life carries the cheapest interest. Where I was born, the reality of everyday life resembles Russian roulette of the "street bank" versus the ordinary people. It is always hard to think of South Africa, the country that birthed me, with wide open spaces, glorious sunsets, and the indomitable spirit of her people who surpass suffering circumstances—now only to bear the undisputed crown since the 1990s of "crime capital of the world."

Want, not need, requires gratification, sometimes instant with no required credit rating. On the *bank of the streets,* you don't need an evaluation to see if you are good or bad. You can just walk up, present the loaded debit card, and effect the withdrawal. Click, point, shoot. Rogue cell, dis-ease, panic, and the ensuing confusion of inevitable change. Life is not a popularity contest when it comes to selection, but we have—and still do—perpetuate a world without unbiased spirituality.

While many writers have expanded on this world as three-dimensional (body, mind, and spirit), I still see us functioning in 2-D: the mind and matter scenario. It's nicey-nice to think that we live in a 3-D world where at least 40 percent of us really care what we are doing to the environment and Mother Nature. What we do in reality is elect leaders who will continue to affect the status quo. No one really wants to seriously consider the mass impact of life without fossil fuels, and there is not, at this time, one in the mass who breaks through the wall of ignorance, saying, "This is how we do it, folks. Let's stop trying to qualify why this has happened. Let's get on with it."

It's grand to think that most of us are spiritual in some way, that we as humans do not have the slightest inclination to dominate and control, to beat and harm (whether physically, psychologically or emotionally) those from whom we sense opposition or weakness. Our world is full of people who remind us every day to stay within the limits of control, and we are surrounded by the justification of righteousness.

"Justification of righteousness?" you ask.

"What about the money?"

"What's the big deal?"

"I have more than a few bank cards, customer appreciation cards, and flight miles collector cards, and yes, the customary almost-maxed-out credit card to complete the lineup. If I have to worry about something at 3 AM, it may as well be that. The tax man is waiting in the wings to build new roads and schools on my behalf, so I have to work to make sure that I contribute to society."

Otherwise I am a washout, right?

"I've gotta contribute, man."

Can't be a washout, renege on the responsibilities, and cheat whatever system, for the very nature of that thought is against what the very fiber of existence is made up of. Keep the job you hate, smile at the boss you detest, forget the dreams of childhood you once had, and put the bumper sticker on the van. You know, the one that reads *"I owe, I owe, it's off to work I go,"* which will reinforce to everyone who reads it the humor of reality and the fairy tale that created the division between you and your partner in the first place.

We find ourselves in the five sensory states of humankind; to see, hear, touch, taste, and smell governs all of our experiences. We are having the same experiences in familiar pleasure and pain that those blinking Egyptians found almost 6,000 years ago. The same ones who are now mummified into silence about their tales of love and loss, their struggle against the tide and the unknown of the future that threatened their entire civilization and took them beyond the brink of extinction. Who would have thought? We have a pretty long tradition of seeking out the sensory experience of life while ignoring the intangibles, don't you think? Why change if it has worked for us for so long?

Imagine *The Plan*:

Let's take the fundamentals and holy books from every religion in the world and build churches and temples around them, to segregate people, you know, to keep the masses under control. We'll tell the people that each one of their religions is the only one true religion, and each respective God is the only true spiritual light, their savior or prophet. We'll make up effigies and customs and tell the people that they are in charge of watching out for one another. That way we won't need watchmen, and if anyone veers out of control, we will give their leaders the indisputable power to evict, burn, maim, and kill those who get in the way. We can shroud that in a democracy and tell the people that they elected the leaders in whatever form it takes—so they got what they wanted. Just in case the people get too liberal in their thoughts and start taking their spirituality into their own hands, we will read the most horrific tales of persecution and torture from the oldest stories in the books to reinforce by showing them how harshly they will be punished. For good measure, we will take all the original manuscripts where the original teachings were recorded and hide them away, and if prophetic messages or unusual things appear to people, we'll hide that information from the inquiring public as well. The *piece de resistance* will come from the exclusion of the female co-operative leadership roles and feminine intuition, and place men in the front and center to control everything with definitions, logic, and the mind. In addition to this, why don't we only select movie and television scripts that prescribe to the norm, just to make sure that no one is going to think outside the box? Let's jam humanity's brainwaves, silence the scientists who know what happens to our brains when we watch television, put one, two, or three of these transmitters in every household, and brainwash every nation into our way of thinking.

"How will we do that, sir?"

"With fear."

Sound outrageous? Wondering where I sucked that one from? How is it that entire nations of upwards of 30 million people have been controlled for more than 150 years, believing "their" own superiority and righteousness over other entire nations?

We needed something that would reach millions of people with a unified message. Bing-badda-boom, I present the television. TV isn't bad, you tell me; it's educational and there is a lot of good stuff on there. I suppose that you are also going to try to convince me that each one of us has original thought during the 9 PM screening of the Academy Awards, or whether or not the guy in the murder investigation is really guilty. TV is great for those people who escape into it, avoiding the actual issue that their subconscious is crying to them about the state that their lives are really in. We don't want to see the truth. We search for it, but when life actually responds, we hide. Think of your favorite soap opera, the harmless one that you watch while ironing, and the one that has been running for five seasons or maybe more, that has you excluding any other activity in favor of the addiction of finding out "what happens next."

We are addicted to the drama, aren't we? Boy meets girl, girl is separated from boy by some evil plot, and the struggle ensues to get them back together. It is the repetition of the good versus evil horror plots of the world of fairy tales, a place where it is better to look back and fear the Witch of the North than worry about the fact that your partner has gone to introduce him- or herself to the hot new neighbor. I think that this is our fascination with weddings, too, where we finally look at the gown and the glory of the moment, and somehow feel that the struggle is over—that the good guys have won over the bad guys. The drama, like our lives, continues to play out, and the storyline that follows human interest, which is marketable and popular, never changes.

Newsflash! Goodie versus baddie has been around since someone took the Christian idea that Lucifer fought God and won over Earth so that God could eventually send a massive army under Chief of Security *Archangel Michael* down here and toast the dark angels' ride.

When are we going to outgrow our addiction to bedtime stories and start fighting the demons in the cupboards of our lives? I don't know about you, but I personally haven't seen God come down and blast the gang who is dealing drugs to the neighborhood nine-year-olds. Or the gun runner peddling rusted ammunition and AK47s to a fourteen-year-old army? The humanity part of me does wish there was some Big Bad Daddy that pops down here with the giant wingspan and automatically knows who the bad guys are and fries their asses out of the frying pan.

Boom!

Bye-bye bad guys, hello peaceful lifestyle. Just like in the movies!

"Did you see the one where the action hero travels all over the world with these nifty gadgets, and survives every situation with a brainy idea, and gets the baddest guy in the end before our world explodes? Oops, we forgot—brains and bravery melt the resolve of the hottest heroine to soothe his every scratch. Cool, eh?"

We all want the baddies gone. We don't know, in our real world, what they look like, but they gotta go, man, whoever and wherever they are. No pressure on me to know my next-door neighbor—if he really has psychopathic tendencies or not—because some Big Daddy is going to toast him one day. The bazooka of spiritual gurus is going to get them, therefore I don't have to concern myself with it. We all have an alternate sense of accountability, in which we superimpose our views of justice and forgiveness on something other than who we are. Are we really forgiving someone for a transgression, or are we following a set of guidelines set out for us? How angry are we really with other people who have hurt us, and how do we compel ourselves into a compassionate disposition when it doesn't really exist within our psyches? Silently we are storing unforgiveness, fear, and anger, and manifesting it in a large storage box labeled "Denial," which can be dealt with when we have time, or when life gives us no other option than to deal with it. Do you know what we are wishing for here? Every day? Every day, every thought that we have about retribution is going out into the atmosphere of our creation to encourage that which we fear the most, *Armageddon*. In every religion and culture, we are faced with the same conclusion to our world: Big Daddy is coming down to fix the mess and straighten it all out and make it nicey-nice again. So, if I get this straight, as humans, we wish for the very thing that is going to destroy us, our blue-green beautiful gift of this Earth that we have inherited, and life as we know it. When are we actually going to look within ourselves and realize that within each one of us, light and shadow exist equally, and it is within our free choice to choose which of those we wish to explore in this or any lifetime? It is only with the challenge of the shadow that we are able to move toward the light and it is with the acceptance of the shadow within that we lose the fear.

One afternoon during my meditation, I had spent hours in a deep rag-doll state, reviewing my life and going through a regression into my childhood to find the weapons to combat a now-tiresome, recurring jealous streak that I was experiencing in my personal relationship. During this experience, I went back to the "Hall of Self" as I call it now. I wanted to see all the personalities that I had created to survive in this lifetime, some of which were halted and stunted at different stages during my evolution and development as a soul on the Earth. It was during this time that I realized that life is harder on us than I had experienced. Crazy statement, I know, but to me at the time, it was groundbreaking material! To think life is easy is a human expectation that is not only impossible to achieve but ridiculous in principle. We are not here on holiday. We are at times so unprepared; it can be likened to playing in the PGA Masters Tournament with three clubs. We always get to choose which ones we want to play with, but it is nine clubs short of what we need. For those of us divinely inspired, the rules of the game dictate we can have two more if we are really ambitious.

During the meditation, I became aware of something moving in the dark, slightly to my left. I was deeply engrossed with contemplating my rejected innocent child-self and helping my teenage self out of sexual torment when this black image finally materialized into a woman's form. To say that I was frightened is the understatement of my life, but I was focusing on this form, who I figured to be some evil power sent to suck out whatever good was left in me. With all the terror in me, I still found myself strangely attracted to the power this image had. In my usual fighting mood and up for a challenge, I shifted my focus to the darkness and felt myself merge into this being's thoughts, and started to view all the bad, anarchical, and dark things that had been part of my experience to that point. I felt the hate, the jealousy, the anger, the fear; the control and the darkness of seeping nothingness embrace me like a wet shirt. It was mine. It belonged to me, and at that marked crux of my life, there was nowhere to run to, baby! I had nowhere to hide. This was me. As the realization dawned on me, I felt a cold sweat seep into my bones that even reading *The Amityville Horror* through a nine-year-old imagination couldn't have mustered. As I began to see through this inky blackness, I felt that each and every emotion I had labeled as dark or negative was not coming from the outside world, but from me. Sure, I had had bad things happen to me that weren't my own. This was different.

"What if I was so negative that I was covering my tracks by being good and through my denial of self was actually attracting dark dramas into my life?"

"Nah! Can't be!"

"I'm a Catholic. I pray every day. I'm good. I'm safe."

The darkness didn't leave.

I prayed.

I began to tremble in an effort to find a way out of the elephant dung I was standing in that was me. My thoughts of people's jealousy, anger, hatred, violence—it was all there. All of my hidden thoughts were in me, sitting in the dark like a leopard waiting to be let out of its cage. I panicked. I had to do something. But what? I was immobilized.

It was then that I began to feel the sorrow—for not looking inside me. For all the judgments I had placed on myself and others in the process. Most of all, I had begun to think of God as self-absorbed and ambiguous. How I had viewed the Creation as trite, unimportant, unidimensional, and disconnected from everything else.

I had to get out of this place and think.

I dragged the two parts of me like a wounded knight into what light I could see, trying desperately all the while to distance myself from the thoughts in my head. I knew that I had to do something, and I reached out to this equally powerful side of myself and felt pity. I felt the pity that I feel when I see someone who is without love, and I knew the darkness to be just that: without light and devoid of love.

I lay in my bed and wept for three days. It was as though facing my shadow had given me a reason to love myself, a reason to change and begin to mutate into wholeness. I began to think that perhaps facing your shadow self was a key to heaven. I felt somehow relieved and lighter; more connected with the struggles of life and the world around me. I began to feel a deep compassion for those people who can't move themselves into the light, ever. The dark of ignorance, the feeling of being stuck with no option out of a hole. Perhaps choice is the only power we actually have, and everything else is bullshit. We try for power over others, but that is control, and so not authentic power. We can make money, but that fortune is tied to so many variables that we have no control over it anyway. Fear is the only thing that manages money, the fear of not having or fear of losing what you have earned. Choices can be motivated from any emotion. So, in that choice moment of dark or light and the ability to move from one to the other, lies the only authentic power we have to shape who we present ourselves to be. If choice is the key to heaven, then we should start using it. The only reference I could find about any keys to heaven is that God apparently gave them to St. Peter. I'm thinking that maybe he locked us all up here, hid the keys within us, and buggered off with the map.

Perhaps our DNA holds clues of how to unlock our true selves, and with every unconscious breath we take and every unconscious thought, we make a decision for or against life. How long are we going to walk around blindly before we realize that we are all contributing to the eventual destruction of everything we know to be reality? We are all living in the lie that we perpetuate in the same way we criticize our teenagers for irresponsible behavior—"*They think it will never happen to them ... until it does.*" Then we bullshit ourselves into thinking we are in charge and that our world does not reflect anything.

Some days I think of Earth and our plight here as a paraphrased urban legend: "*Our parents went out for a stroll and by the time they came back, we had moved.*"

We told ourselves that we didn't actually need them. Then we told the little ones that Mommy and Daddy had left us alone, and the older ones would take care of them. It was a mess. There was only one guy hanging around with a broom, made of broken soul fragments, but hey, he looked harmless and sort of floated around. Some of the children took comfort that there was at least someone to watch over them.

The older ones started fighting about who was better equipped to lead the little ones. Some bright spark in the bunch said: "Hey, guys, I have an idea. Let's split up. That way we can all lead the little ones."

What seemed like a good idea at the time became a nightmare. We were all afraid when the dark came. We thirsted and we hungered. We all cried for our parents. We convinced ourselves that it was they who left and not us who wanted to be autonomous and test our wings without someone constantly correcting and helping us. The cover-up started and the deviance was running thick and fast. We could perhaps tell the little ones that Daddy was working in some other corner of the universe and on important business creating stuff. Ahhh, but the inexcusable truth of a mother leaving her children, that would be hard to console the babies with. We had to make our dirty deed look good, because in eternity, we would have to make up excuses why God and the mother aren't here. We would have to say we didn't believe in parenting. We didn't believe that we were actually loved anyway. We couldn't look at the fact that we wanted to experience autonomy and power. The lamenting didn't stop.

"But why, oh why did Mommy leave us here alone?" cried the babies.

"She had other things to do. Maybe she went with Daddy."

"I have the answer for you," said the Voice from the shadows. "Women who leave their children are not women at all. Women are supposed to support, love, and nurture, keep the family together. There is only one description for a mother who deserts her offspring."

All the children listened.

"She's a whore."

All of creation went quiet. For a minute. Then all hell broke loose.

A little voice at the back broke through the pandemonium and said: "If our mother doesn't love us and she's not coming back for us, what are we going to do?"

There were now some confused rumblings.

The little ones could understand a father having to create and go about fatherly things. But a mother? Besides, the Voice had a good explanation for her behavior, in that mothers who don't conform to the norm are wa-a-y out there!

A few of them turned to the lurking face in the shadows.

"Please, sir, tell us what to do," came an older voice.

There was a silent pause in the darkness. A tacit chill blew in, followed by the flapping of thousands of wings.

"There is only one way," came the advice.

All ears were now tuned.

"Burn her. Pretend she never existed."

So began the days on Earth of removing the mother and everyone who resembled her. The voice with the bone feathers coached and soothed where he could, waiting for his "plan" to take shape. He was armed with something that the little children had no defense against. Ever. With this one chess piece now in place and with the father and mother gone, shut out by their own children, who now believed in their own self-sufficiency, their own dominance, and their own brilliance. All of which they reveled in, patting one another on the back in reinforcement of small victories and encouragement to do more. The next move would be so easy.

Like taking candy out of a child's mouth.

A boy and a girl were talking. They were from the older clan. She was not happy with the counsel that the voice in the dark was giving. She still believed that the mother would come back. She was also gaining influence among the more sensitive children who missed their mother and made sculptures from clay to remind them that she lived.

"What are you two doing out here on your own? Shouldn't you be tending the little ones?" The Voice was stern.

"We will join them in a bit," said the girl, eyeing him with disdain.

"You know," came the Voice again, "I have information about your parents and about how this all came to be."

Hope springs eternal.

"You both look tired, hungry, and worn out. Before I tell you, you should have an apple."

The Voice. The collector of soul bones. The interceptor of light was armed with one important weapon that makes atomic physics and nuclear weapons look like water pistols.

Guilt.

So, in closing this story, the cycle of demobilization had begun. When the children cried, they were told to stop. When they were suffering or sick, they were unacceptable and needed to be killed off. Guilt fixed all of the woes. Guilt replaced love as pity. Pity became caring. All babies who cried to their mother were hushed, classified as weak. Emotion of any kind other than instinctual survival was frowned on. Intuition and emotion resembled the mother and her, well! We all know what she did! The father's attitude needed to be emulated because he was a Creator and provided in an invisible way for everyone. Law, order, policing, dominance, and silence. A world where the black and white ruled. Everyone was hurt. Stories of love circulated around the fire, idolizing our father who was working somewhere else while we silently torched the mother.

We have all bought into a fabulous marketing campaign; accept what your world is coming to because you are powerless to do anything about it. As a woman, you are powerless. You, as a man, are powerless. Someone has the power. We don't know who they are, but they are out there. They must be, because who is actually running this show if the "someone" isn't actually there? There are a bunch of people in charge, but they got a wee bit confused with the terminology—serving the masses became amassing somewhere along the way.

The simplicity of the veil of ignorance and knowledge, the veil between here and hereafter and the veil of illusion is that it shields us all from the realization that we are all part of the problem if we choose it so. Little do we grasp how much development is actually required in our psyches right now, and what sacrifices that particular change would demand of us. Here we are, plodding along in the path of our lives, not even conscious of our decisions or how we could empower ourselves, still deeply engulfed in the "destiny" and "what is meant to be" formulae that disempower us all. We keep pulling the plug out of the wall when we need the light the most! Be that as it may, our decisions require of us to move from one close circle of friends and the work that we may enjoy to another, in search of meaning and acceptance. In our little dramas, we are left with nothing but our still-miserable selves and a lot of emotional debt. We look to romance with temporarily resurrected hope and vigor to solve our "never-ending fairy tale" problems. We all want to love and be loved, to be normal. Any dissolution of that becomes equivalent to abandonment, which leads to fear and anger, repeating the cycle in turn. The fear and anger, in any expression, leads to loss of control. The denial of both can put you on a slippery slide with our old standby, depression.

Most people tend to look from a subconscious level at their partners in an alpha male or female role, and when that partner chooses to change and continue on another path, they are seen as abandoning their mates. Oh no, we can't have a change of heart, people! Even worse, fall out of infatuation or love. This is a crime for which you will be buggered up for the rest of your life. You have to commit forever. This is the definition of love on this planet. Didn't anyone brief you at the gate? After the abandonment has settled in and had a chance to soak in hurt for a while, it re-emerges with shiny self-righteousness.

"I'm better off without him."

"She wasn't good in bed anyway."

In the profoundest manner, we embark on the matter of retribution, taking justice into our own hands with the unique ability to take one's weakness and use it against the perpetrator. Sun Tzu's *The Art of War* is a fine example of knowing thine enemy's weakness and using it against them. Of course, being in a relationship, we are now armed with closets of weaknesses of the other party. More so than the shoes she bought when she was with you. Now in retribution, we start to lose control in our lives, which inevitably leads to tears. We humans hate being out of control, because at the bottom of the control barrel, there is nothing left. Once the fallen leak into the barrel of self-pity, where the many tears were shed, the depression sits and stares back at you in the cocky, "Hey, so-and-so, what are you gonna do now?"

The only solution is held in the formulas of the white coats, and begins with wailing and lamenting,

"There is something wrong with me; fix me and heal me."

We pour out our broken lives in little segments on the table and get a prescription to fill for each fragment of our broken souls. If there are more tears, then there will be more painkillers. Days and weeks will pass, and at some point, there will be too many tablets to take at different times, and when we can't remember who is actually in control because it definitely isn't us, through the drugged haze of our pain and how many tablets to take, we take them all.

For those of you who are thinking that the bottom of your barrel is too dark right now, I would like to shed a little light on what it looks like from the other side of death. I am not speaking here of an out-of-body experience (OBE), because too many great authors have shared their stories on how and why and what it looks like. I believe that death is as different to us as we are to one another, and that no one theory is right for everybody. Our deaths are as special as our births, and our individual departure from this life can be as simple as leaving our physical bodies and not feeling any change in existence other than leaving our five sensory perceptions behind. I have simply found death very devoid of our human experience. You are alive. You are dead. Get over it. What matters only is what you are doing here, why and how you do it. To look at life through your beliefs and get on with it before you excuse yourself through ignorance or fall asleep in this class or get left behind. I would like to talk about the death that we really forget about, the death that is the *in-your-face* transformation, the living change. This is the part where you get to write your own chapter as the main character. Where the person you look at one day in the mirror is no longer there the next. For all of us, writing our own chapter is terrifying because we will be laid bare if we screw up. It will be lying on the floor for the crowd to see and comment on, so we buy into the "someone else is in charge" scheme. But death will happen to us. Something is going to change. We have to pick up that pen and start writing!

I had a lifestyle once upon a time. I was a medical specialist's wife, who drove a minivan and had the two beautiful children and a home I would have envied, had I lived next door. Immigrants to Canada in a mass exodus of professionals escaping rampaging violence is not without its tribulations. I think that in the rosy retrospection, I had it all, but being there at the time was an uncomfortable experience. I existed, I had no identity, and I served no other purpose other than basic household chores, my husband's dreams, and going to church every Sunday. I woke up one day and realized that there was no love. I looked for it everywhere—under the bed, in the basement where I had packed last year's snow gear, the dirty laundry basket, and the archived "inbox" folder. I packed my two young sons up after the customary witch hunt of marital and spiritual counselors and a piece of paper from a lawyer who said I was able to live on my own. We agreed over dinner that we were both to blame—which appeased our righteousness—and went off on our merry ways. Hope and faith were prevalent like the snow that year. I was used to double-checking with someone else all the time, and I felt control slipping. It started with dinner. It became late. Sometimes the pizza guy would deliver our food. I was slowly catapulted into making decisions alone. Financial ones for the first time, and I now also had no one to tell me that I looked fat in the pink dress. I had also left the confines of my spiritual home, where my dusty Bible lay beneath a quiet cross. I was then immersed in the modern-day Christianity, where all sorts of cool things were going on. Good things, God could see and you didn't have to explain anything. All bad was caused by demonic possession, and my personal woes were caused by rebellion. Confusion reigned matchlessly, but I still needed something to fix me. All this change and free-radical stuff had moved me into a definite broken state, or so I figured. I tried the self-extraction of the demons to get rid of my rebellion, and I was considered a risk in those days, being a separated woman. How could anyone love a woman who had chosen to love a man and then go back on her word?

In front of God?

There was no room in the house for sinners of this type. What do you know? Those demons kept coming back, and my spirit fought me for the light, tooth and nail, until I wound up depressed and gray as my life seemed. I know that three out of five people today suffer from the helplessness syndrome called depression, so you know the blackish grayness to which I refer. You can't go back and you can't move forward. The air around you is thick and heavy. Forgotten memories plague a routine grocery shopping trip. You can't speak, because as soon as you open your mouth, the wailing from your soul takes over. Opening your eyes in the morning is reason enough for the tears to start spilling out. Sleeping is the only solace, if you can, because there in your dreams are the faces of the past and the face you are not. For those lucky people who have not experienced the feeling of being glued in walled blackness for what seems like an eternity, I do not recommend you take a crack at it.

It is, as human experiences go, probably one of the most repugnant. I used to call it *"The Dark Night of the Soul." I didn't realize that there are tales from other people describing their journey through the darkness to move back into the freedom of self and the true lightness of being.*

This leaves me to ponder why so many of us choose this route as a way to self-discovery. We elect someone to be in control of our path from birth, to the point that it doesn't work for us anymore. At this crux, we decide to take the reins in one fell swoop, but we have never had the reins, so we don't know how to steer.

"Whoops, man, this car is outta control; gotta stop here."

We find we can't control anything anymore, and we are definitely in the true definition of the meaning of being out of control. We cry inconsolably, unleashing the pent-up emotion of all the years of suffering, and we have direct experience of the apathy that we really feel for where we are in life. We start to see the real pointlessness to the "lifestyles" we are creating. Boys and girls, welcome to your first class on looking through your veil into reality. God forbid we actually think that depression is the first step in the right direction. We have to con ourselves first, and I resume my story.

So, true to form, I think that I am crazy. There is no purpose to my life, and that I am not a spirit created by the light in the image of God. I am just a dumb human being who can't get it right, and after all, what is the point of this fiasco anyway, and who will miss me when I am gone? *"Nobody loves me."* This would be my personal favorite of the victimized cries for attention. Why didn't someone tell me that I was supposed to love myself? Wait, I remember now; self-love equals conceit and conceit equals bad girls. I wanted to be a good girl and live happily ever after; this equals no self-love, equals no self-respect. Respect is for people to sing about. So, I take all the pills at once and wind up in my head, semi-dead, wondering if people would say nice things about me after I was buried. Look at how far the delusion goes. Now this is the part that no one really wants to talk about—what happens when you are so out-of-control that even the death you create with your own hands is a failure. Where do you go to from there in your ego? That's all this melodrama is really, a battle with your ego and your spirit. The little ego that thinks it's a really big deal, full of pride and bravado and no real substance to speak of.

"Piss 'n vinegar," my grandmother used to say.

Anyhow, my big ego thought that it would teach my spirit a lesson in reality about who is really running this show. I guess my spirit showed my little ego a thing or two, and had us both committed to a mental ward. Nice thing that, the old id and ego versus the unexpiring spirit. "Ex lifestyle inhabitant" mother of two sitting in front of the professor of psychiatry, trying to pass tests I haven't studied for, and trying to convince him of my sanity. Sounds simple, but if you consider convincing the judge of your innocence while you are in jail and all your rights have been stripped, it gets a little more complicated. Especially if he's an *uber*-white coat who knows more about what's going on in your mind than you do. Then, if ever there was a time in my life I believed in demons and seeing things that didn't exist in real life, it was on that depression ward.

I recall lying in bed one night, thinking of my would-be religious conformist friends, trying to drive the demons out of me—which, apparently in my rebellious state, wouldn't work; it only drove me deep into the caverns where they breed. I think that mental instability and depression wards are spiritually devoid places where the mind has become the dis-eased tyrant and run away with itself. I feel that mental instability is a kind of childlike state of absolute indulgence. You can be whomever you like, sometimes five people in a day if you choose. You can quote the Bible instead of answering any direct questions, and if people don't listen to you, you can scream at the top of your lungs about God and His wrath, and fire and brimstone. For those of you who don't believe in God, you can always choose the "garlic-around-your-neck option." This one requires a dress code. You need to wear black, and possibly depending on the level of your delusion, the same clothing for however long you choose to be incarcerated. Next, you need to find the knotted-together, twisty-viney garlic that you can wrap around your neck in long strands. You can even pretend that they are pearls if you like. Anyway, without giving you more creative ideas, the most important point here is to mistake everyone you meet for the vampire who is coming to get you. This works on your roommate really well. You can't pick your friends in "mind jail," but if you stay long enough, you will find a paranoid cellmate who will find you absolutely fascinating at 3 AM. My roommate provided the same endless fascination for me at around the same time. Bounding up, whipping curtains back, and yelling at the top of her lungs: "Stop staring at me!"

Generally, this had an immediate effect on my adrenaline levels. It would snap me out of exhausted sleep I had fallen into after listening to young girls going through their personal hell of detoxing off some drug they thought was cool, in a bath of ice one floor below me. The irony of it all was that I felt sorry for them.

It was then that I was given a key. I saw the strain on the visitors' faces. I started to see that all this self-indulgent crap I was putting myself through was actually exerting control on people who actually loved me. No one visited me there, and frankly, I didn't blame them, as it was not equivalent to a day trip to the mall. I saw one thing that appalled me, however: It was the very people who seemed out of control who were in fact, controlling others. I saw myself in the shoes of my apparent oppressors; in my human weakness, I was really turning this anger around and controlling the feelings of the people who loved me, and sucking the love out of them, instead of them giving it freely. I saw it in everyone's eyes in the group therapy sessions. We all sat there. Guilty. Our mental fates served to us, a cold dish in the hands of depression. Some with scars around their necks. Some with healing lacerations on their wrists. Me? I had been given a clean bill of mental health, but my wounds were still seeping on the inside.

I fumbled against "promising not to ever try this again" and wondering, as I packed my cosmetics to go home, how the hell I was going to be able to explain this to the rest of my world. As I walked into the icy-cold sunlight that day, I felt like it was a new beginning for me and I had brought along my only friend, guilt.

Humbling experience—not to be repeated in this lifetime. If you are sitting reading this and thinking from the black hole of your turning point in your life, don't run from it. Volunteer in a mental-instability hospital, and you will very quickly see that this is not a true path for you to venture on. Look at your depression as the light going on, not out. Look at it as a new way to see the light. Bing-badda-boom! If you don't see it that way, find a white coat to help your journey into the light.

Remember through this all that medicine, traditional or modern, has its place in your recuperation but at the end of it, you and only you have the power to change. We need to move from the diagnosis stage through the state of fear and panic which is so human and normal to us that is seems like a natural conclusion. We have to sit back and assess the situation and how we are going to move forward into growth and wholeness. This is what it's all about. It is failure that creates within us a need to succeed. This is how we take the hook. Is it that we fail and then try and do better next time or is it that we err on purpose to learn from the mistaken situation? Trial and error or failure to succeed? Now, not all of us succeed once we have failed, mind you, but we attempt once again to climb the ladder.

I used to meditate a lot in my younger years, and learning from practiced masters enabled me to find solace and understanding in the quiet times when I closed my eyes. I have spent a lot of time during my life contemplating my world within and the reality I am experiencing. For many years, either as a young girl in church or later when I practiced many forms of meditation, I found my life more pleasant sleeping or lighting my candles and doing my contemplations. It may have made me more peaceful afterward, but I really battled with the peace within and the duress I experienced when I moved out of that state of perfect equilibrium. I had better knowledge of my breathing, which helped me scuba dive. Perhaps I missed the point? I found that time of my life to be most difficult to master, even though I graduated in technique.

One particular experience stands out for me today when I think back on those arduous hours with no circulation in my legs. During a meditation, I had visions of my guide, who is an odd-looking fellow; he brought me to a huge library stacked from ceiling to floor (which I believe was about fifteen stories high) with books amassed with knowledge that has been, is, and is about to be in the entire universal consciousness. I think that even in the meditation with the openness of my spirit and not in the smallness of humanity, I could see what a daunting task it would be to yell out one day, "I want to read all the books in this library!"

I think that forever would not even be close enough, and then where would one store the knowledge afterward? The point was, however, that I in that infinitesimal moment "felt" like reading all the books in that library.

Mortal human, eternal soul, wanted knowledge. All human souls are part of the greater search for knowledge—enlightenment—and the ensuing changes the information can bring you. As much as we feel that we know all we need to right now to keep us moving forward, there has to be a striving for greater ease to enable any growth. Most of us strive for knowledge, graduation, and the eventual accreditation that one particular section of knowledge affords us in the end. Even though that may be the end of our lifetimes on Earth, it only heralds the ending of one book and the beginning of another. It is in this vast library, which I consider the "Universal Library and the Center of Consciousness," in which possibly all knowledge exists.

Inspired fatalists look at creation of music or art as re-invention of what has previously been put out there. Perhaps tapping into the same train of thought, if we are all connected, is how inventions occur on the other side of the world simultaneously and another's action sparks a chain effect of doing things, like the inspirational parable commonly referred to as the "hundredth monkey" syndrome.

We are somehow creatively in avoidance of finding new material within our souls, so we look to an impetus to discharge energy and keep us moving. We also need to be aware that deep in the shadow of our souls, our other self exists, and when we create, we find our dark selves before we find the finished project. I think that we are realizing that the circle is finally closing in on us, and that we have to start turning the circle into a spiral before we get sucked into a vortex. Perhaps there are some theories out there that describe this in better detail, but in the quietness of my own mind, I believe that if a circle is opening to its greater potential, then it is growing. When it reaches past the three-quarter closed point, the velocity will run it to its closure, which is inevitable and then spin out into a spiral or spin into itself in a vortex. Either conclusion is full of dynamic potential, both being equally as powerful in their outcomes. Our geometric masters will tell you that a circle is complete unto itself. Pick up a pencil, a compass, and grab a piece of paper. A circle is a circle. Begin here. End here. Same thing. Yes, dear, perhaps in the 2-D world, where everything on a flat surface has a logical outcome. Explain that to me with your spirit!

Spirit and matter are the two utmost ends of creation that exist within you as you are sitting reading this text. Spirit creates matter, and matter enables spirit to create. The Creator created light; light became you with the help of the Creator's thought and love process. You became matter. Whether that is light matter as spirit or material matter as human form is choice. But here you are nonetheless. You need to realign yourself in the Creator's image. You are born to create and you desire creation. So in order to create, you move to matter and you begin to create. All thought is creation in action, and combining that with love, you have the recipe to bring into reality anything you desire. Manifesting creatively is not that easy, though, and if it were, you and I would be sitting on a beach in Jamaica, sipping coconut rums with all sorts of dead folk, fairies, and angels. Our lives would not have dividing walls of reality and veils of spirit to keep us segregated and craving for more knowledge. We do have one thing in common right now, in that we are matter, made up of all the atoms and carbons that is the dust of Earth. Let's imagine for a moment, the Creator took five planets in five universes and made them into "free will" zones. On these planets, we get to choose to be anything or anyone we like. Heck, if we don't like who we are at the time, we can change ourselves along the way too. Poor, rich, famous, disabled, homeless, believer, atheist, blonde, brunette, male, female, superman, or anarchist—am I getting my point out yet? The fact is that we don't think that we have the choice. We see ourselves as disadvantaged in some way or another. Poor suffering souls at one end of a solar system where there isn't evidence of anybody else except remnants of great civilizations that knew everything and buggered off with the knowledge in a puff of smoke and light. The only people who think that we are interesting are the aliens from a distant galaxy, who travel zillions of light-years to perform lab rat tests on us. Woe is us! Our leaders have gone crazy and our lives are a mess. Woe is us! We are poor human victims of poor planning, and now look at the state of our world. Did you choose your sexual orientation? Did you choose your partner? Did you choose your career? Did you choose your life? Did you choose circumstance or did it choose you? If you qualified any one of the above statements with "yes, but ..." then you need to look at who is really in control of your life.

"Who is really at the helm of your ship, Captain?"

You say you are, but you whine when things go wrong and you are unsure and doubtful when they go right. "Cautious," you say. "Realist," you qualify.

It's bullshit, I tell you. The bullshit that you are continuing to believe and buy into that you are not in control of your life and not in control of your own destiny. You used to believe in fate and destiny. Those two things ran my life every day for the first thirty years of my life.

"Them two were gonna make me rich, famous, find me my soul mate and I werz gonna live happily everly after, I tell yerz now."

If I had five cents for every "what will be will be" statement, I would be rich and famous. Damn, I'd even be on TV! Everybody could see me then and say the same thing day after day, and maybe they too could be rich and famous. We can all put every single drop of energy into that statement and never have to get out of bed, or get the kids to school, or say *sorry* for anything. "It is what it is." Like the lottery. Take the coin out of your pocket and put it in someone else's pocket—never wondering where the money really goes—and spend three hours to five days magically building castles in the sky. Magical wishes that take energy and thought and creation. Spinning up, up, and away into the atmosphere away from you, away from your center and your life and your dreams. Bing-badda-boom, look at that! Someone else won the 5 million!

Now you can pack your magical castle away with all that energy you so magically created and sent to your family, buying the affections of those in debt, turning it around into a second of negativity, and zap it to the poor, unnamed, faceless person who won. I always find it strange that people wonder how they lost all the money they won on the lottery. Maybe I would start with the fact that it has the negativity of 5 million one-denomination coins attached to it and that every time someone sees the face behind the lottery marketing campaign photo in the supermarket, the thought "that money was mine" flashes for a brief second through our heads—and sitting on top, for a great ride, is the prime emotion of jealousy. We have all been creating negatively in our lives without knowledge or cognizance of this for centuries.

For those of you who believe you spent time in Atlantis, you should know what you are headed for. This legendary continent apparently suffered under a misguided society, where one side was intensely spiritual and the other was purely emotive. The two segments didn't meet and everybody was intent on making the other side see their point. There was no acceptance that both sides were right and could integrate to live in harmony. It is in some circles inferred that the power of control on either side, similar to male (spirit and logic) versus female (emotion and intuition) energy conflicts that we are now experiencing, is what brought the house down.

The Egyptians and the Mayans, on the other hand, were very aware of the powers of creation and they used both in very purposeful and unique ways in their civilizations. Egyptians segregated a select group of individuals that the Pharaohs had serving them in the temples as architects, medicine people, artists, translators, and linguists. Some theosophists have said that these "elect few" were from another planet. Others have defined them as enlightened gods. I agree more in part with the latter statement, but I propose the following: a group of scholars sitting around under a palm tree, navel-gazing. They are experimenting with new ideas and different formulas to preserve and uphold the current reign of the kings of old, before King Tutankhamen's reign circa 1361 BC. To paraphrase, the king has told them that he wants his statue and pyramidal empire to be the biggest ever. The weather is harsh in the desert, dates are dry, and primitive tents are not much to keep the sand at bay. Being buried in a tent was no way to live back then. Some bright spark falls asleep in the sun and starts to recall the ancient art of alchemy—transforming one matter into another—and realizes the potential of that creation within human beings. He starts meditating, and during this tedious process, starts to see the power of being connected with all forms of creation. He enlightens himself.

Intelligence and enlightenment are the spark of divine light, and that light cannot be contained, so it lights a fire in everybody around.

Suddenly the affected few rise within the group with amazing powers and abilities to perform wonderful feats unseen and unheard of before. We witness the birth of the magician. The holders of poof and wielders of mirrors. The more the confidence builds, the more work is being done, and the "regular folk" look upon the "select few" as gods. Heaven forbid they think that they could do the same thing themselves. The pyramids are erected and kings are buried with piles o' cash. The ankh survives as the only symbol connecting the dots scattered down the banks of the Nile, along with the hieroglyphics as a photographic map and the misplaced Rosetta stone to unlock the door. Poor Egyptians, we say. Wonder what happened? Such power, such knowledge—buried under all that sand. The world is full of relics of misused power, and we are the saddest of all of them.

We are the unused and then misused civilization. Sure, we got power in hydro-, carbo-, geno-, electro- and solar. We've teetered and tottered with nucleo- too. We've been out there blowing up crap—the ozone layer, the Arctic, the Antarctic, the bottom of the sea. Heck, we've even blown one another up for shit's sake. Human life is cheap. There's more where that came from. Bing-badda-boom! We've got more excuses than memorial epitaphs for all the people we've killed, and the only thing that we are really proud of is our differences and that we can blow the crap out of anyone if they even try to fool with us. How about those Mayans? Archaeologists predate Mayan culture to the tenth millennium BC, but we have *proved* that they were around about 3,000 years ago. They seemed to be in such a hurry to get out of here, they forgot to pack a few things that we keep to remember them. They left their calendar, which we still follow, but even *that* is about to expire in the year 2012! This has a few of us scared witless, but thankfully not on the epic-fear proportions of Y2K. The Mayans also left us a few bits of furniture and kitchen appliances. We call those "artifacts" now. In studying some of this stuff, I start to wonder—if these past civilizations had something to stay for, why aren't they around now? They all seemed to have lasted between 2,000 and 5,000 years. Ahem! As scholars navel-gaze under our trees, we have come up with some conclusions:

They blew themselves up with explosives, in some sort of war, overtaken by famine or consumed by disease. Perhaps they were stupid, intelligent, brilliant, or evil. Or they were "taken" by God, the devil, or extra-terrestrials. They went home because Earth wasn't that cool anyway and Mars had a new drive-thru coffee store they wanted to try out.

The point is that we are facing the brink of being extinguished by our planet. They were not. This is the only marked time in history when something this global has been predicted, by science and spirit, to happen.

We don't really want to hear about love, do we? Love is an excuse to have sex, isn't it? Sex is good, and we can all just get along with blowing one another up tomorrow, if our neighbors piss us off again. The one thing that we are most concertedly here to learn is the one thing that we cannot face. Jesus Christ came here with one clear message, the rest having been thrown into the washing machine of mere mortals arranging life into neat little sectors that have been segregated to form modern society. Paraphrased and translated, most other messages are not distinct and are from accounts of the time He lived. He came here to say one thing, and one thing alone: "the greatest of these is love." This He added to the already tabled form given to Moses, called the Ten Commandments of God. Kind of like "Appendix A."

This is where the Atlanteans and Egyptians fell off their chairs. The power and control was too much fun. Hey, it's much more pleasurable to have a "slave for a day" to do your homework or your housework than have someone stare into your eyes all day and say "I love you" so that it reverberates through your soul. That is the moment for most people when, faced with love, they look at their watch and rush home to feed the dog they haven't got. I think that the early Roman Catholic Church had the patrons' number on this one. Some poor repentent parishioner came to church to confess, and the priest passed down the words: "God loves you, go and sin no more," the guy looked at him and said, "Huh? Is that it?"

But that wasn't it for him, and he had to go out and do it again and again until the village folk got sick of the behavior and stoned him to death. The churches got smart and implemented the "Say Hail Marys until you are blue in the face system" and it worked because you had to count on beads until your knees ached in repentance and sorrow. As humans, the way we have been is that we have to see and feel punishment. Sin deserves punishment. "I have been bad and I deserve to be punished." This is the result of control. We have not been in control of ourselves, so we have put someone, anything, everything else in control of us, and we wonder why we are so miserable. We know the difference between right and wrong. It is part of who we are. This is why we are remorseful. We transgress from everything we know is right, because if we were in control of ourselves and knew ourselves, we wouldn't do it in the first place. We transgress because we know that someone is going to find out. Someone is going to go ballistic. Someone will hunt us down. And someone will punish us for what we have done.

Case in point: You don't want to be with your partner anymore. The situation has degenerated to such a degree that you can't even stand to be around when they are breathing. Their smell infuriates you. You can't at this instant admit that the once-perfect person standing in front of you is exactly where you really don't want to be. You embark on a path of trying to amend it. You find new friends to whine to. You find the arms of someone late at night to ease the pain; all the while, you are looking for a way out. Somebody has to move the chess piece, so the nightly arms of solace become the excuse. You know hell is facing you, breathing fire down your neck, tearing all your personal belongings in two with its claws. Rather than admit the truth that love has escaped you—again!—it is time to don the detective's hat, dust off the cloak, and go in search of love. That elusive bandit!

We stereo-typify and create borders from which we can securely lock ourselves away from the harsh realities that exist outside our gates. The gates that I speak of are the gates in our minds. The ones we have built for our safety and keep the unpredictable outside, where it needs to be and referring to it in recognition as a "scary" or "evil" place not to be ventured into. We have used religion, culture, and race to create divisions of safety. We hide behind laws that have been created based on a human interpretation of spiritual laws. We have become so good at the process of interpreting thought that we don't even know that we are doing it anymore. Process then becomes thought, whose final outcome is the transformation into matter. The reverse is true with the learning process; matter transforms to thought and then into process. Many of us have read books that upon questioning, we couldn't remember the author or the title of the book, only that that book changed our lives in our thoughts and actions. Is it not the same with television or movies? We allow interpretation of what occurs outside of us to transform our own thought patterns. This is how human thought patterns can change for the better or for the worse. How do we really know what is happening on the streets of New York City right now? A major TV network's news broadcast? What about that African AIDS crisis? What about the Iraqi war? A politician's view of the status quo? What about the international status of terrorism? We have an idea of what is going on. This is not reality. Somewhere we lost the power of creative investigation. We prefer someone to filter through the information for us, summarize it, and spoon-feed us in the quickest way possible.

The Internet is the unbiased bridge from which we can fish, cross-referenced in a sea of knowledge, and draw our own conclusions. This requires a lot of groundwork and a lot of reading—if you are interested in finding the truth, that is. You could start looking for the truth inside yourself. Have you been bullshitting yourself as the networks and media have been presenting news as entertainment to us? News is not truth anymore, it's entertainment. Of course it's easy to believe them when the last thing you want to do at 10:00 at night is look at yourself and what decisions you are making every day you are alive and well and living on planet Earth. Where do we start in the washing machine of what is going on in our heads at this time? As a *pro forma,* I will take a leap and say that the thought flashing through right now is a tie—the fear of change itself and the belief that nothing can really change.

Change takes commitment and continued commitment to improve what you have. That is, if you believe improvement can happen in your life without sex, drugs, and rock-and-roll.

We are so used to looking outside of ourselves for the cure that it is a natural conclusion to a common problem, personal trainers, psychotherapists, bankers, managers, and stylists. The proverbial Yellow Pages of self-help. Ever look inside the Grey Pages? The grey matter of real good self-help stuff situated between your ears and behind your eyes that costs nothing but a five-minute chat every morning and night that would be the best thing you have ever done, but don't trust. You and I trust everything but ourselves—other people's opinion of us, whether we are going to succeed or not, whether we are fat or thin, whether we are "normal" or not. All of these decisions rest in other people's idiotic minuscule opinion of a human reaction of a soul on a lifelong journey. We listen, though. We think that these opinions count. We allow people to beat us, demean us, and degrade us, who we are and representative as souls.

I may not have been an Egyptian goddess of the Nile or in love with Alexander the Great, but I am my own soul on a journey that is incredible *to me*. I may not be able to convince or change your belief system with tales of exorcism, reincarnation, blessings from the pope, pilgrimages to Mecca, or the re-invention of people after serving in wars. I am what I am. I am human on a journey to completion, as you are. We are no better or worse than one other, and the sooner we see our spark within one another as a whole, the better for us and the easier our evolution will occur, which is upon us. I have not served in a marked battlefield, nor have I been someone famous. I do not think of my life as being wonderful or leaving a mark on someone or something—these are the dreams I had as a teenager when I was not witness to the death and destruction that we as humans are capable of. It is time that the negativity can be eradicated in its tracks, in creation, and in our minds. How often have we said the following statement? "Isn't it amazing how sometimes the very thing we are afraid of or said we'd never do finally happens to us?"

In the order of thought, your subconscious, or "Sub" as we will call it, knows what you desire as a soul to grow or just to teach you a lesson, perhaps to humiliate you or show you that your judgment of a situation was in error. You don't want to listen to the old Sub. That would make you really unpopular with the neighbors, so you pipe up in conversation: "How could he or she do that to so-and-so? I could never do that to someone."

Two years later, you are rushing to your car with half your clothes in your hand, bright red with embarrassment, wondering if anyone saw you. The Sub pipes up with a flashing subtext—the judgment you placed on someone else in the same situation two years earlier. Humbled? Some of us get to have our photos in the news while others get to challenge the societal face of disdain. How could we do that? Especially after knowing that it was wrong? It's like the Sub preplanned the downfall and you and your conscience are left to ponder who is really in custody anyway. Maybe the communication you are seeking in your relationships is actually your Sub speaking to you in tongues. There is someone there that you need to get to know if you want to stop from sneaking down the road of life half-naked and ashamed at your recent fall from grace.

Lessons in our lives are just equal reflections of what is going on inside of us. To start with, imagine yourself as this giant family living within a community, a country, a nation, a world, and then the universe. If you are having a problem with communication in your relationships, is there something that your subconscious wants to tell you? I am not going to recommend meditation or your local yoga class as a means to get in touch with that. For some people, an injury or sickness, or a vacation alone will enable the conscious and the subconscious to meet. For the deeper spiritual commitment to take place, you need a daily routine of this communication to become more fluent. Our spirits are gentle and can't really be bothered with the rough-and-ready attitude of our conscious mind that has run amuck with logic for the past however long it has taken us to get to this point of returning. They need one thing alone to coax them into staying with us and helping us out of our human dilemma, and that is love. You are not going to buy, pay, bully, coax, force, or shed the inner self into joining you in this journey. There is nothing about you that is human in any way that is going to enable your spirit to kick into your life and help you. You may even find that your spirit has left you a note since you have been disconnected from you for so long that reads, *gone fishing*. You may even find that your spirit and the life you live are so far apart that it may even be pissed off at you. Not your average welcome-home present!

Most of us think that we are attached to our spirit and that our spirits are alive and well and functioning in our everyday lives, and that each and every "good deed" that we do is spiritually enabled. Well, dear folks, if you are anything like me, once you get in touch with your spirit for real, you are in for a little shock. The ego has a clever disguise, and it is called the "we don't really want to go into the real spirit communication" mode. Otherwise known as the "we are doing fine on our own, we don't need any interference" staple diet of reality, and the "look how good we are because we do such great stuff for other people" egomaniacal behavior. You always know when this mode is kicking in when you feel justified and seek credit in denial mode. I knew that the old ego was trying to divert me when I wanted to buy the bumper sticker that read *"practice random acts of kindness."* The fact that I wanted to advertise that I was practicing random acts of kindness and put the "la la look at me" sign on my vehicle meant that my ego was once again behind the wheel. Roadkill! I was, in fact, just another human being having entirely selfish motivations in trying to perfect my tactics and nudging my soul into growth here on Earth.

I think that we have bought into a very warped way of looking at ourselves, especially those incarnating as women in this lifetime who suffer more from being labeled as selfish. How horrible. Terrible. Just the uttering of that word against us sends most of us into an inner spiral of torment and self-prejudice. The word "selfish" has been used against us as a weapon to counteract any thought or action that can be misconstrued as moving against the motivation of the person or group to which we appear to belong. The dictionary spells it out as an adjective meaning to be concerned mainly with one's own needs or wishes. It goes naturally against the grain of being "Zen" and singles us out as not being a "team player" in that we are looking out only for our own gain. In a single word, we can reduce individuals spreading their own influence in their own world down to feeling unwanted and insecure about their core values as a soul. Isn't it funny? Pathetic, really, how we as humans, in order to control one another, never attack the action but rather the soul. In praising one another, we rarely praise and uplift the soul. Instead we praise the human, appealing to the whims of the personality to flatter and bolster the ego. I think that we do this because it motivates and facilitates the system of control we have in ruling order. News flash—we are all selfish and are mainly concerned with our own needs and wishes. If that were not the case, we would all smile in traffic because it makes the driver next to you feel good. We would know our neighbors. We would buy grocery hampers for the local food bank and we would appreciate our family as gifts, rather than property. Self-preservation is: *the protection of oneself from harm or death.* If you have been living under some Sword of Damocles in your life or that someone else has imposed with the "selfish" hilt in order to coax you into a destructive cycle or convince you of your worthlessness, then I urge you to take a long, hard look at the situation.

Our world is covered by a veil, simply the veil of ignorance that descended on this Earth in some point in our history as humans, and it's gotten thicker as time has progressed. Let us imagine for a moment that we are living on this beautiful Earth and being in total control of our spiritual, mental, physical, and sexual selves. All four of us cozily wrapped up and functioning in perfect order and firing like a high-powered sports car. Contrary to popular belief, I believe that growth occurs without strife, because love and light are limitless and so is the Creator. We cannot limit the ends of growth, because if we grow in love, we will continue to expand forever. So, here we are in this perfect world and everything is going along in a calm and peaceful manner. For those of you familiar with the biblical Garden of Eden, I don't remember reading that all was well in the Garden and that Adam and Eve were chilling out with God and communing with Him, but they were bored because they weren't learning anything, so they actively sought out Lucifer to put a little spice in their lives. Nay, people! We were doing just fine as a human race at that time. We were conned into thinking—and have been thinking that way ever since—that it is in the control and domination of one another that we grow and become whole. We believe that the guilt, terror, and fear in which we actually function are habitual, and that is how we have always been.

We exist in a perpetual state of "ancient artifacts of truths" striving for wholeness. We hardly ever ask if it there is another way, because it doesn't seem to be from the point of empty resolutions we feel powerless to change. We are whole! Just as a kicker, there was never anything wrong with us in the first place, nor has there been since. We have had just about everything and everyone tell us that everything is wrong and that you need "such and such" and "so and so" to make it better. We have been taught that through strife we grow, and this enables other people to tap into destructive energy and tap into that as a power source. Think that's bullshit? Have you ever watched a couple having a verbal argument, and one person manages to find the lever in the other that switches that person into the energy-giver mode? You can see the energy draining out of the one and moving into the other person, and I am not talking metaphysically here, because most of us have not developed our human eyes to see beyond the physical. You see the "drainer" become more flushed, and their stance improves, while the "drainee" looks dejected and gray, and their stance moves to protect their gut or solar plexus area. I feel worse for the "drainer" than the "drainee" in those circumstances, because they are just repeating a tale that is so boring and old, and the person who has chosen to co-create this in their lives again. The "drainee" is actually the one with the authentic power. Ask yourself why anyone would try and drain the phony stuff? Thieves don't steal things that are worthless.

Now I just want to add something here that those of you who think you are justified in this mode of behavior need to look at more closely. You are co-creating this scenario for one of two reasons: One, you think that you are "helping" the other person because they "need" you, or two, because of karma. Karma is open to belief systems and interpretation, and not always reliable in the way we access that information. Realistically, all you are doing is perpetuating a really fascinating old game, like chess. Two people engaged in the combatant duel until someone else wins, while watching your opponent's body language and tapping into the "rules of war." It's a mental game of supremacy. Most board games are just that—the total fascination and use of one's intellect and skill to outwit and maneuver the opponent into submission. Anyone who's ever won a five-hour game playing Risk cannot yell "I won!" without a victor's gleeful sneer. Humility in competition is an oxymoron. Making more of us into morons than others, but we engage nonetheless. I don't think that any one of us enters a competition "just to be there" when we are all there to measure our successes and failures against one another.

This is also true for applying to the ever-competitive job market. Where else do we have a chance to pit our skills and our experience against one another in a race to fill a job position? Perhaps this is why we obsess with death as the ultimate judge, taking our lives and measuring them as success and failure scenarios. We try to pray our way into a better seat, cheat with age-defying miracles, and just generally try to outwit death by skirmishing all the way. How can we cheat the final closure to this life? Why try to do this when the very thing we are here trying to accomplish is the integration of all of our selves and mind, body, and spirit and the abolishment of all forms of human domination by control accomplished by allowing more love into our lives? This is change. The dual carriages that block the realization of our true selves through change are guilt and fear.

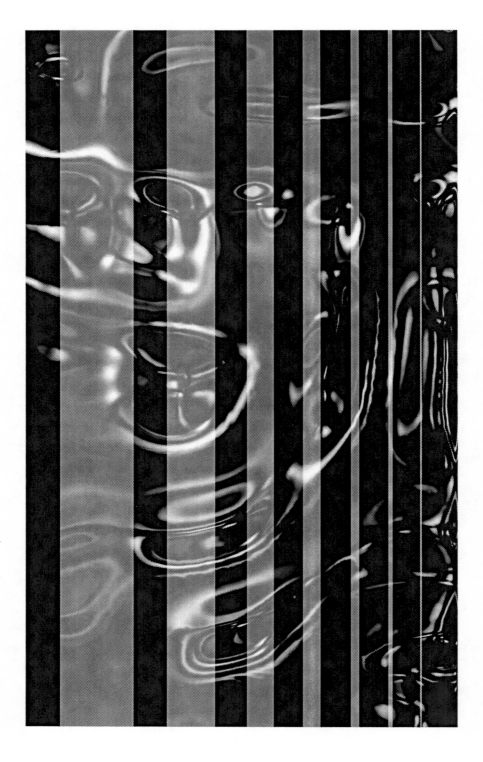

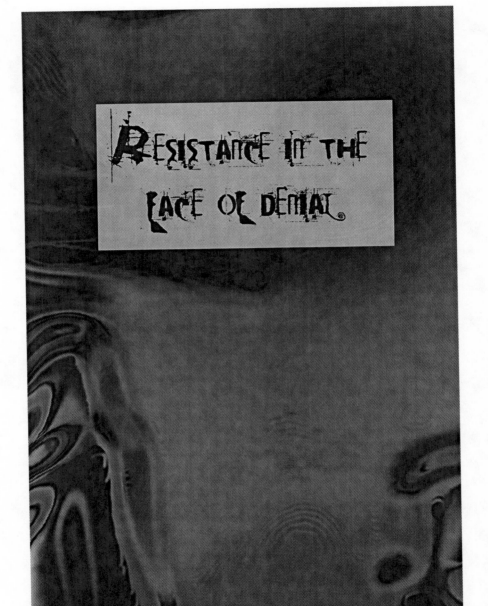

RESISTANCE IN THE
FACE OF DEMAT

WE all have it. We are all unified in our denial of its existence, as well as our universal acceptance to paint fear as existing somewhere other than in ourselves—or our part in creating this every day in our minds and projecting it into our lives and into the lives of others. Some fears are bigger than others, and some are so big that they run the program. The magnitude of fear in our lives is not measured by how weak or how strong we are as humans, for this is a purely human measurement system. It is by how much we as humans give way to fear in every area of our lives. We allow fear into our lives in the first place when we buy into the thought that we are imperfect or simply being less than anything else. This is because we are functioning on a three-out-of-four-cylinders-firing syndrome. Our spirits are being excluded from the program, and our personalities are running amuck. Ego is tripping along nicely through its adolescence of invincibility, when it realizes that there is something bigger than it and it is outside the human form. Heaven forbid the ego, now in fear of being found out for the fraud it actually is, acknowledges its master, the pure spirit. Sometimes the fear presents as sibling rivalry, creating dissension in families. Most of our fear manifests as abandonment, insecurity issues, or feeling lesser on the scale of love than you could be.

We buy into these drama cycles for the rest of our lives until someone throws us a lifejacket that reads "I'm OK." We fear being set free into a sea of contentment, and we switch our energy to fear of rejection as a lifetime theme. We then project that into every relationship, so that when it backfires on us, we can retreat into the only saying we know that will get us any pity and absolve us of any responsibility for any injustice created by ourselves against ourselves: "I wasn't loved."

The only person who never loved us was ourselves, and relating our story to someone else is like giving them the keys to our entire existence.

"So-and-so didn't love me, abused me, disrespected me, ignored me, hated me, attacked me, etc. Therefore, I am here today, this victim of poor circumstance that you see before you, assailed by fate and the *winds of change.* That person made me who I am."

I realized my pathetic reluctance to take responsibility for my own life when I was trying to blame my lack of commitment on the fact that there wasn't any in my childhood. I recreated this scenario in the people I chose to associate and have relationships with, so that I could continue to reinforce the lack of engagement in my own life. I become conscious that I am a whole person capable of commitment with others, but I was limiting myself to the early childhood exposure to another human, thereby dictating the way I experience my life for the rest of my years. Most of the time, we believe that change is more painful and upheaving than it really is. My favorite definition of the word "change" is moving from one system or situation to another. You get up in the morning and instead of the brown shoes you always wear with those jeans, you choose the black ones. Choice is the greatest gift that this world has to offer. Imagine this Earth as a zone where anything you want exists. You are the creator of your life, and you get to choose, and that choice enables you to change—daily if you like. Whoever told you that you had to stay the way you are, with who you are, was lying to you. Free yourself to choose. Free yourself to change.

If you are looking for a point to all this, then I would suggest the following: The point to life is learning to be self-reliant; being totally dependent on oneself for the source of inspiration and the creator of situations that advance our individual growth without the desire to control or be controlled by any emotion or drama that involves anything other than love. Of course, there are some with intent in this world who have totally the opposite in mind—there are malicious souls who dedicate their long and tedious existence to destroying and creating harm as long as forever and ever can be, to creating evil. I do truly believe that not all of our experiences on this Earth are of our choosing. There are people with no other motive than to create guilt, fear and anger in the world. Perpetuating dissention and harboring existing trigger points and dividing families, countries and nations even further for their own destructive gain and not for the good of all. There are truly horrible disasters occurring every day to innocent victims of circumstance.

These circumstances involve the following modus operandi: beings that are strolling around Earth with nothing better to do with their creative abilities than perpetuating fear, anger, hatred, and the darkness of ignorance. These are the souls who take it upon themselves to take the essence of life and destroy it. I have seen them crawl at the edges of darkness, eating on the scraps of an already-fearful human being. Already disempowered by society, hungry and devoid of human rights, these people wake every day to a world lacking anything that remotely resembles love. Woe to the maliciousness, when the six billion-plus human souls finally wake up to their own potential as creators.

"You think that we don't see you maiming and disabling souls with terror, pain and suffering you inflict, at will, on them?"

You exist in the darkness of ignorance and supreme intelligence, and you are without light, in any form. You outsmart and outwit those on your trail, for now. Your time has come to be brought into the miracle of knowledge and love. Humanity is facing its own wake-up call, and even though we at this time don't feel we can do anything, there will come a time when we will all stand up together and yell "Enough!"

We as a global society, all one in the spirit without being together in a group, are going to rid you of your ignorance as we face our own. Together we will all face the light and you will be forced to return the innocence and the life that you stole from each and every one of us. Call it a reversal of rights management. We are choosing now to be in charge of our own changes. In pure love, we are on to you and we are no longer going to choose to be your victims. We are not going to ignore those who are choosing to be victims either. We are going to realize that in love, we have the best defense system going, and the only casualties will be those who absolutely cannot live in the light of information, accountability, and responsibility.

In the structure of our world, we have created walls to segregate society, and in some nations this system is still functioning as a means to control. Cause and effect at this time is the experimental energy force of change created by a group of light beings known simply as the *"Family of Light."* This is a common spiritual term used to describe a group or family of thoughts working to bring about enlightenment. They can be both human and non-human in form, and together are collaborating to bring about changes in light energy on the planet. In a non-human form, as angels perhaps, together with humans, the *Family of Light* can bring into matter that which we have as humans forgotten how to do—or are too afraid to bridge. In esoteric values, encouragement and strengthening of the soul can help further a mortal struggle. It is within "bridging the gap" between our reality and a world of light where all that is dark has been exposed to the light, that global effort is most needed at this time. We as humans are going through a confusing time, trying to discern and integrate all of the information coming to us via books and television regarding planetary and human changes, and let's face it: The path is rocky and uncharted. This is all part of the plan, because it is time that we found out just what our own truths are and not those prescribed to us in the form of judgments, doctrines, and dogmas. Enough is going on in the houses of formalized religion right now, exposing the truths previously hidden in monasteries, convents, and schools of learning. Right now, one religion in particular is facing a rough time sponging down blood off the walls surrounding their altars. Isn't it enough of a crime that religions have purposefully withheld teachings from us and the gift of teaching within their walls for more than forty-nine centuries? It is also a time for the rest of the religious doctrines to be aware of the judgments that they have placed on one another, because their time is coming too, and their faults will be exposed to the public as well.

It has been said—albeit too much with the "fire and brimstone" warnings—that, "in the end times what has been in the darkness will be exposed to the light." I believe that this will come to pass with all things as we here on Earth become less tolerant of the bullshit and start expecting the best not only from ourselves but from one another. This is in truth and light. Up until now we have been no more tolerant of one another's failures than the witch hunters of the 1600s. We search and dig and scan for the shadow in one another until we find it and then hold it up for everyone to see. This is the control domination we all play a part of when we collectively "cut someone down to size" or "bring them down to our level." This is most especially apparent with our music and film stars. It is as though we build them up just so that we can break them down again. Isn't it enough that we have forced them to seek the leadership and limelight by having them "pay their dues," by not "giving someone a break." We idolize those for the longest who have the greatest flaws; those who battle with their weight, either under or over, or with severe addictive, emotional, and physical problems attached. We see them as more "human" that way. We collectively sense that this person is at our mercy and we can, at any time, slap their face on the front cover of a newsstand magazine with a derogatory slur attached. Sometimes we do and sometimes we don't "because we like them." We certainly don't want "free-thinking, brutally honest, intelligent, and beautiful people as our leaders". These people are a threat! They would eventually show us what frauds we all are, hiding in the dark, waiting to pounce on them via the artists, X-rated Internet touch, or a jilted ex-boyfriend from thirty years ago. Ah, people. We created 'em cookie cutters for a reason.

"Either you're in or you'll have to wait in line with the rest, because I am in control here and I say who gets to be the next superstar martyr. *Capeche?*"

We have suspected this all along. What we haven't realized is how we all play a part in this human drama and how we are all connected with energy and life; together with our thoughts and emotions, they combine with energy to manifest our lives and the world around us. Still think I'm off my tree? Look at the divorce rate. Horrible! Sixty percent of marriages in North America end in divorce. So we choose to live together and have a half-assed commitment with one another that we can both just hop out of whenever we want. Perfect. When last did you witness a couple getting married—the groom, the bride, the cars, the dress, and the flowers, the families gathered with Kleenex in hand and think anything other than, "I wonder how long that will last"?

You have just taken all of your denied feelings of fear, distrust, and disappointment in the whole world and dumped them on a couple (no matter their age), doubled with a huge dose of powerful emotion, and given it to them as a wedding present!

In the process of getting married, a couple may interact with close to two hundred different people. From the circle of friends, to the engagement period, house hunting, wedding planning, to the final day of the wedding, when lots of people see this couple. Kaboom! Whether or not you believe in the marriage ceremony is not the point here, as most of these ceremonies are still being done through the religious rites. It is important that a couple formally commit to one another in the wholeness of a balanced relationship in a light family. People have become ashamed of being married. Rings are optional. Some last so long and act in a way that testifies defiance of the odds. Couples divorce all the time, due to many reasons, including my personal favorite: irreconcilable differences. That is exactly what it is when two people split up. Men and women are different, but they will at all costs try to build the white picket fence, and when that fence gets too high, it's time to bail. There are honestly some things in this life that are not worth dissecting or subjecting ourselves to further punishment. We are never privileged enough to find out exactly who, and sometimes what, we are coupling with in the first place, and all sorts of things go into the decision to choose a mate. Then there is the whole messy business of portraying ourselves as something that we are not. None of us has ever done that! Yikes! That is something that other people do to fool us and trick us into loving and giving of ourselves, our sexuality and our money. Some of us will be lucky enough to have all three happen at once.

Trickery happens because we don't know who we are in the first place and need someone to complete us in the areas that we think that we are lacking. When we start to explore love in a relationship, we buffer ourselves up against our partner and start looking at ourselves through that person's eyes. It is then and only then that we begin to see what we are made up of. Sometimes this partner brings the worst out of us, and sometimes the best; in either case, this is how we learn. We can live on our own most of our lives and be perfect. Hell, even the neighbors like us! Get together with someone and kapowee! A destruction and demolition derby. Why? It takes the energy and interaction with one another as humans to bring our light and shadow selves to the forefront. This is why we as humans choose relationships as our learning ground. It is earthly relationships and the sexual nature thereof that are used in this way. We find each other in a myriad of souls and learn from one another. Some of us learn the lesson and move on faster than others, and other relationships are just destined to last a lifetime, as those two souls have chosen to interact with one another and the world in a coupled fashion.

I have read many theories about soul mates, and even more disconcerting is the fixation on the perfect mates and the meeting of same in this lifetime, often waiting for their arrival before becoming coupled. This is a much-hyped concept, the one of soul mates, and deserves a little consideration. We think that if we meet the perfect person who will be able to read us and respond to every wish before we know what it is, we are going to alleviate our emotional growth cycle. We need to experience growth and interaction in order to get where we need to be in a perfect relationship. This is like thinking that we can skip the crawl cycle so that we can just walk. Can any one of us think that we are so advanced in this life as to skip the laundry and get on with the enlightened stage? We are destined to be adults here, intrinsically interwoven with our human forms, grounded on the Earth and the Earth in us. Any of us who think that we are going to bypass the time we need to take at really looking at who we are is in for a sorry shock. In forming human relationships, we are all in a common belief that we have to do things the way we have been taught, shown by other relationships that we come into contact with and situations that conspire to "keep us where we are."

It is never that way in a whole world. It is not the way that things are supposed to be in a reformed society. As it stands at the moment, we continually thrive on dramas to keep us afloat and make us feel alive. Some people thrive on jealousy, anger, and violence, while others flail in human disease, embracing illnesses and creating victimizing situations that constantly have mental boundaries that prohibit us from moving on—both physically and emotionally—into healthier relationships, whether that is with partners or friendships. We always take the easy way out. We will find one crutch to replace another, just as we are learning to walk. It's as though we say to ourselves, "Hey, I'm finally getting the hang of this," but two days later, we're in another relationship, which is often harsher than the first because we haven't dealt with the problem in the first place.

"But I love him or her, and I can't afford to live on my own."

"He's/she's not really all that bad; you just have to get to know them."

"So-and-so is just having a bad day."

Therefore, we excuse the abuse. We see ourselves as deserving of this treatment. We think that no one else would love us in the same way. We have become addicted to the negativity because someone "loves" us enough to put us in our place. Love has no drama. Love has no control. Pure love is not addicting. It is not abusive. It just *is*. Whole relationships are built from the ground up, centered from the acceptance of self, respect of choices, and the power they have to shape your life. In the love for another person, in whatever way the relationship develops, you continue to strive for all these values with communication, setting personal and joint boundaries, and cooperating in forgiveness and compassion. Each person has a unique vibration, and it is up to the two people to either build the other up to their authentic potential, helping them when they fall, or to destroy everything they have achieved and stunt their growth.

Most of us sit and let life pass us by. Our lives can be stinky and we know it's stinky because every time we breathe, it smells, but it's a comfortable smell. We never try to change the modus operandi, especially not within ourselves. Heaven forbid we should actually admit that we are indeed 50 percent of the problem *and* 50 percent of the solution. If you have walked away from a relationship with a feeling that you did all you could with love, and you can let that person go into someone else's arms to be loved as they should, you have accomplished the goal. Everyone is free. You are borrowing their love and their time briefly to learn all you can from them. Some relationships may last longer than others and so what? It's no loss that you were with someone for three weeks or three months, and neither is it if you stayed for thirty years. The fact that you are willing to love and accept love and be open to the challenges and change that a relationship brings is the victory. If you are carrying a lot of anger and hurt around from a relationship that ended in a way that you were not in control of, I suggest that you look at your motivations at why you became involved in the first place. Was it the classic fairy tale that got eaten by an ugly troll? Was it because you needed something from someone and you never got it? Your emotions were arrested in a certain period in that relationship, but you are now stuck in that time. This is all you can think about, and all your motivation is centered on "payback time." Your car, your new partner, your vacations, your new job, and so forth all have the common motivation of "Look at me now. Look how great I am doing after you dumped me." And the world-famous, "I'll show you."

You gotta look inside there, babe! You gotta check the gauges before you go flitting around the world with untamed, unbridled, and undirected anger. Before you do anything else, you have to let it go. Let it be. You did not own that person. Even though that piece of paper told you that you bought some property in the name of love and cemented the deal with a strip of gold, you really have no right to it. It was not yours to start with, it wasn't yours during the relationship, and it is not yours now.

What are you doing with your life in the meantime, while you pine away and stick pins in the pillow at night? I know at this time all you can wail out is "how my life is meaningless without him or her."

I think that this should be the time that you look at yourself and start getting in touch with your soul and your spirit, because they are mighty pissed to hear that you don't care about anything except another human whom you had physical contact with a few times in a lifetime. If we are thinking that life means nothing to us, perhaps we should start looking at the life we are creating for ourselves. We are so hell-bent on punishment—"they'll see when I'm dead"—that we are being sucked into the darkness all around us.

This is the time to bail, baby! Grab the life vest. Take a swimming class and dive. You are precious. You are an individual part of the whole that makes up this life for all of us. We cannot allow you to go on hurting yourself and others in the pain that you are content on creating over and over again. Let it go. Breathe and let it go. Don't make it more complicated than it is.

You may try to get something right, and just when you do, someone has to tell you that there is a bigger and higher step to leap before you can get there. *Evolution*, they call it. *Progress*, they call it. *Nonsense*, I say. Everything is perfect the way that it is. *Just perfect.*

One of my teachers tried to explain Sir Isaac Newton's law of gravity to me, which went on for days. I was a distracted student. In frustration, he grabbed an apple from a lunch and hurled it out of the window. The whole class ran to the window just in time to see the apple explode on the cement corridor two floors below.

"See that?" he said. "That's gravity."

Boom! Like thought and energy. Both very simple transferors and simple in their process.

When I started trying to visualize a better existence for myself and better relationships, I began working on the creation of such through my thought pattern. I was working on a lack of commitment in my relationships. Looking inside, I meditated on all the areas I wasn't committed to: work, friendships, and general daily activities. I was doing things without being present or focusing, not really caring about the outcome or really where that energy was going after I was putting it out. It was amazing to me to see the many things that I did without even noticing. I began a daily battle with myself and the mantra of changing the pattern. My mind resembled fried spaghetti halfway through, but I plodded along with the following:

I will be committed to everything I do today.

"But what about if so-and-so does this-and-this?"

I will deal with it in a committed manner.

"Yeah? But last night we had a fight and I don't feel like dealing with anything today. Can't we start tomorrow?"

"This is too hard."

"What difference will it make anyway?"

"If I change, will he leave me? You know what happened last time."

"I like my life the way it is."

The last line is what kept me in the non-committed fashion for more than three decades. To tell you the truth, I hated my life. I floundered into different jobs, learning different things, but I always lacked a sense of staying power or commitment to anything that lasted too long. Well, it took a long time to realize that even though I was a risk-taker, I lacked courage for myself. I could risk anything for a paycheck or a "you're great" slap on the back, but I could not risk taking a chance on me.

"The world is not waiting for me; let someone else do it. Plenty of good people out there; go tell 'em to do it. I'm quite happy wallowing in the mud of self-desertion here, bud."

I was so dis-easy with myself that I couldn't sit down for longer than thirty minutes in deep thought. I'll keep mediating and reading and doing self-restoration because I've got a war going on inside of myself. Call me if you need someone to market the finished product. All right! That was then and this is now. I am now having too much fun to be counting how long the process has taken me or where it has led me in the grand adventure.

Our world is changing, people, and it's taking us right along with it. I know you all feel it, and all of us are a little afraid at having to jump in at the deep end, but that's not the direction we are supposed to be going in anyway. You can't get to the deep ocean from the shore unless you go in from the shallows. Physical law. Like the apple thing. Simple. Your spirit is in charge and there is no one who can steal it, kill it, or do anything to it unless you allow it to happen.

I remember when I used to attend the Theosophical Society when I was about ten years old, and everything that was lectured about and guided through workshops always had the same credo—that you had to be careful, because you could get "lost out there." Boy, I can tell you that the "out-theres" of the world are many, and I was fearful of getting lost. Most of the time, I didn't even know where I was, let alone trying to find myself a way to come back to where I didn't have a place to be. It took me fifteen years to learn what "lost" meant, and another ten to figure out where "out there" was. These credos were taught back then because people were not told to be in touch with and in control of ourselves. We looked to gurus and spiritual leaders to guide our minds and lead us, often into places that we were not ready for. The most wonderful thing about renewed positive energy and light at this time is that you are in control of your growth. We always have been; it's just that we have bought into the philosophy of "out there." It's all in here. Everything is where you need it to be, and you can tap into it whenever you like, and you're changing, and your growth is your fingerprint, one of a kind. There are no two ways to look at the same situation when you are dealing with two people. It is time that we all started seeing ourselves as the true vessels that we are. We are vases of a sort, each holding individual patterns and blueprints for our successes and our failures in life. Each human experience is individual and tailored to each one of our needs as we require them, and our spirits are there to bail us out all the time. Right-place-at-the-right-time stuff here! You are creating in exactly the right place, so that you can experience being human in a divine way.

What happens when we find ourselves standing on a knife's edge of reality? The edge that I am talking about is the edge that we have all experienced in our lives. That moment in our lifetime when a quantum leap is about to unfold; the split-second decisions we make just before we are about to change paths, directions, careers, or just do a plain about-face. It's the moment before the jury returns with the verdict; the moment of conclusion. This doesn't have to be a conclusion in a revelation of behavior or pattern; it's just an awakening to a different level of awareness. In some instances, though, we refute patience and follow a line into another experience of anger, which leads us to different results than if we have followed our previous pattern. People all over the world are right now meeting with life coaches, guidance counselors, spiritual counselors, psychologists, and psychiatrists to enable the change process to cement in us because in some way we know that the current path of habitual knowledge is pushing us down a road that we don't want to travel anymore.

We all know that we are not alone in this world, and when we reach out into the darkness that surrounds us, there is always a hand that is there to help. The momentum starts with us in our stagnant environment. Ninety percent of our immediate environments are stagnant. Some of us accept it and move within, and some of us rebel against that stagnation. We can all be seen on some levels as bacteria in a pool of water that has been sitting under the hot sun for hours. Some of us hang tight on the surface and maintain a stable balance within, while others split and breed into something that may destroy the entire pond through disease. This state of affairs is what biologists call life. We are all moving toward something in stagnation—some more slowly than others. It is then up to us to look within the blueprints of our designs to see what the patterns hold for the future and what can come of the mutations brought about through change. Our patterns over the past 5,000 years have reinforced in us that stagnation is good. It keeps us as employees, patients, husbands and wives, boyfriends and girlfriends, mentors, donors, conspirators, spies, warlords, dependants, totalitarians, and geez, just about the everything that we are. We don't have to change, because it will upset the balance. I remember my father saying to me one day in my response to his malaise about having to go to work to support us, "What would happen if we all decided not to go to work? That would be total chaos."

Just like what would happen if we decided not to be abused today. Can you imagine? Getting up and saying to yourself, "Today, nobody is going to lay their hand on me. Nobody is going to call me stupid or useless. Nobody is going to tell me that I am not worth anything."

"I can't say that."

"People wouldn't like me."

News flash! If they are treating you like this today, then they don't like you to start off with. They will tell you that they love you because that is what keeps you in the machine and in abusive situations. Be yourself and say no. Respect yourself and your choice. Respect the gift that we have all been given, freedom in choice and freedom to choose and to be chosen. Don't lie in bed one more day and believe the lies that you have been telling yourself all your life that things cannot change. They cannot change because you don't will them to. You have not exercised your divine rights of free will. Maybe I ask you to re-read the Bible before you throw it at me, telling me that it is not God's will to change, but it is indeed "His will that guides us." Nobody knows what God's will is for us, but we follow it anyway. Until He shows up again to bring us from the darkness, we will just sit here and cower in anxiety about right and wrong. He created you in love and in His own image. We have such low self-images of ourselves that we mock, by our very cowardice, the perfect beings He made of us. We are not rescuing the gifts that are hiding inside ourselves. We would rather look to others' gifts and admire those. It is not God who comes in and says, "Where are you?"

No, it is self-imposed denials and the choice to be guilty. We totally negate the love in the world by constantly creating negativity. In every moment that we make a decision, we are faced with two options, positive or negative. I have known very few people who operate in the positive by honoring the moment and consciously making the decision to create positively. We compare ourselves to one another, brandishing clichés around like swords with which to damn one another. When I see this occurring around me, sometimes having found myself in the middle of a hot debate, there are always three fundamental characters that exist.

One is the accuser, the other sits accused, and the martyr suffers in silence.

All three characters exist within us, of course, but I am always amazed how these dynamics play out in every scenario. We are always in some role that places us as the three key figures within the Christian doctrine: Jesus, Mary, and Judas Iscariot. This drama can unfold as Christ and the devil if the players are serious about their tasks. We have the extreme desire to get our point across in a definite way, instead of reaching out a hand in love. How can we do that when we don't love ourselves and we don't feel worthy of any love in the first place?

This is, as I see it, a direct strike against our Creator who had given us individual power to change the world, our world. He gave us choice and freedom and we have created a magi-mix of laser traps to keep ourselves bound and gagged. We love to blame. So we blame Eve, who corrupted Adam. The woman did it! We shame her; we shame her sexuality and her essence. Next, we see the devil behind the plot, so we blame him too. We don't really believe in the devil anyway, but he makes a hell of a scapegoat. Next, we stone, tar and feather, or plain put to death anyone who comes in theory against our philosophy. Just for exacting measure, we will scoop a healthy dose of fear and keep everyone together in close-knit communities and tell them not to stray out of the fold. They will become a lost soul. Damn! Damn! Damn! When are we actually going to get it? We are not accountable to one another in our actions, we are accountable to ourselves. Ooops, I forgot for a second—we don't trust ourselves.

"Can't breathe."

"Where's Buddy?"

"Looked the wrong way today—need Buddy."

It is not the battle with the drugs and the alcohol that is haunting you; those are the symptoms of a greater need within you to show you the way. The longer you leave it, the more you ain't gonna like it, and that's why you keep moving away from what you instinctually know. What you are is the only thing that you've got. Everything else belongs to everything else. Get over it. Get used to yourself. You've got to stop making excuses, too. It's as though we learn at age six how to excuse ourselves from responsibility, because somehow we fear that grown-up responsibility is going to steal our innocence. What is in actual fact a lack of boundaries in childhood—we see the rules and regulations sneaking in to take that away. Before the rules and boundaries are imposed, the whole world is ours and we are free to explore and express ourselves into the surrounding environment. It's as though we live in this haze for six or seven years until the world starts to come into us, or should I say that we start allowing the outside in. Mostly it's the bad stuff that starts to make an impact, because our boundaries are starting to be set, and those have to be imposed by a set of laws that continually challenge us throughout our lives. There are some that psychologically challenge those early lessons and move unscathed into adulthood. We all experience this growth differently, and the same experiences can impact one individual into negativity, yet another may thrive positively. You never know what your soul's reactions to your life's lessons are going to be. Sometimes the very thing you are sent here to do winds up becoming such a struggle that you continue to lose the battle to become more enlightened or wiser from the experience. This is why dramas perpetually unfold in our minds and hearts, because we are constantly challenged by our spirits to face the reality of what occurred and rise above the situation to view it in a different reality. We all, in some way or another, seek love outside of ourselves, but within the darkest part of ourselves exists the alter ego and caretaker.

The "human-matter-emotive."

This is where all discrimination starts, and it starts within the brain early, almost as a programming within the human DNA principles. We differentiate at first between light and dark, hot and cold, dry and wet, and then the process becomes more sophisticated as we use the pathways again and again. These pathways become so well worn that we begin to mix emotion with energy, and our thoughts become projection and intentions, and then our world begins to create itself around us. This process is no more evident than in the early pre-teen and teenage groupings, where we begin to form what will become our adult perceptions and discriminatory processes. Of course, other humans have taught the process to us and we follow their lead, but we get more creative in a destructive way, never even thinking of the possible harm we are doing to ourselves and to our world and ultimately, other humans.

Would you change your thought process if we could prove that your judgment of yourself as ugly, fat, bad, unworthy, or a myriad of other self-hatred expressions would develop co-creatively with other people's, resulting in a world war?

This is why people turn a blind eye to wars, because we all intrinsically feel that we need to lash out at something, perhaps a war to satisfy us. No matter how futile or atrocious in nature, it enables us the expression of hatred for ourselves. I believe this is why we all have the fixation on accidents, blood, and gore. Of course we would never admit to it, because that feeling of hatred and anger is in such denial, it comes out as a deep concern and worry for the injured. If we are so concerned with the victims' well-being then why aren't we helping?

This is also a common theme in post-traumatic stress syndrome, where survivors lament, "It should have been me; I should have died."

No! It is a guilt complex that goes deeper into the fact that someone else died and you were strong enough to survive. If you look beneath the surface, you are actually happy you survived, but that too is in such denial, and it is socially unacceptable to actually be that happy. Instead, you have to accept your part as a victim in the whole horrible crime of death. Why can't we just accept life and rejoice in the celebration of it?

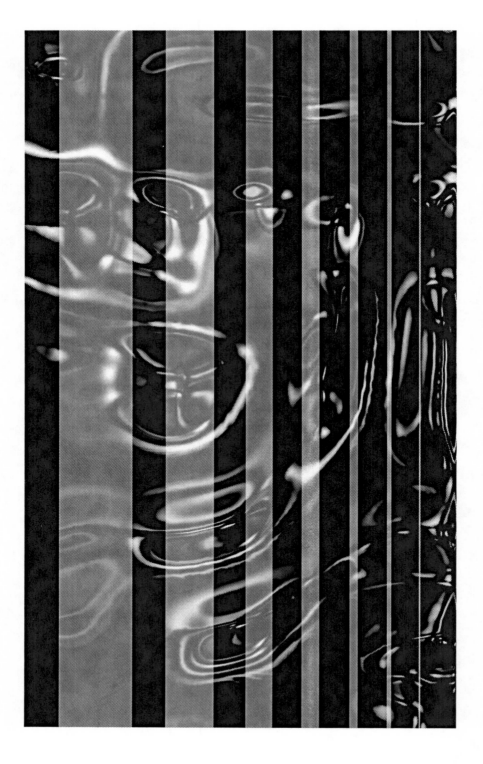

Judgments:
A Definition of Means

WHEN we are faced with a moral or societal dilemma, instead of finding the peace of compassion and understanding inside of us, we look to bring outrageous behavior back into acceptable parameters. We use this in force, might, and coercion. It's easier to send an army after a bunch of reprobates than it is to understand why they are doing what they are. We have already judged them as rebels, so what is the point? They are being irrational. Logistic change takes a democratic standpoint and no one can talk to a half-dressed crazed maniac!

Take the hippies of the '60s, for example, and the ensuing panic that rippled through mainstream society when Woodstock took place. There were a few minor social injuries at the time, but compare that with a protest rally now, and one can see where solid mainstream judgment can take you. In actual fact, if you look at most scenarios, you could do well to look within yourself and ask the question, "What purpose does my judgment really serve me in my life?"

Not much besides the obvious, that you are more stressed out working hard to change judgment paradigms than you would be if you purely accepted the situation. Judging prostitutes is not going to stop them from working their beat as you are reading this. Judging murderers in the Middle East is not going to stop them from car bombing today. Judging sexual behavior is not going to stop innocent lovers from getting AIDS. The only things your judgments are affecting are your peace of mind and quality of life. The only thing that you have to look at now is why you have these judgments and how to stop them from interfering in your daily life, to the extent that you need pills to stop the anxiety or the depression over the state of the world today.

Your judgments will separate you from the happiness you can find in an everyday moment—the moment that allows you to look at anything and see the beauty within. It is only the parables that you have grown up with that shape these judgments and form them into the spider's web that is your framework from which you move away. The judgments of happiness, love, understanding, peace, security, success, and of course all the reverse of that. In its more severe form, your judgments will be in its simplest poison—that of good versus evil. Happiness does not exist in judgments, and neither does love. Everything moves back from a judgment, a line in the sand. You can't be right all the time and be happy. Each judgment forces one to take a side on the line and most often pits one friend against another due to that line. A mother, who loves her child and had been heartbroken by a similar type of guy, finds herself saying to her daughter: "That man is no good for you; he will only wind up breaking your heart."

That is a judgment from the past that exists in one's consciousness that ends up a pattern in the personality: to stay away from long-haired biker dudes. You may argue that this is how we learned as a civilization—patterning. It taught us to survive as ice-men, nomads, pirates. I present a modern world where the only pattern is to stay away from violent people and methodologies with explosives. Personality, when we look at it, is us. It is the defined reality we create, from which everything is born from our experience and how we view that experience. Each person has his or own reality, and that is what we cannot change. Everything else we create from there becomes our reality and shapes the life we live, how we co-create with our outer reality created by other life that we co-exist with. We can change where and when we express that reality, and how, but in the end, it will only be our personality that people remember for a time, and it will be their only impression of us that will last. An impregnable wall of impressions that we created while we interacted with that person or situation at that time of our existence.

For generations, we have subscribed to the pleasure-pain principle, and it is more than time to take a long, hard look at this idiotic idea. Some poet wrote that you cannot have love without loss, and you cannot experience joy without fear. I will not even quote the person who said this, for it is not worth commending someone for a bizarre viewpoint when he had not clearly mastered his own love or joy potential.

One morning, I woke up and realized that I didn't want to create the dramas that kept me committed to the same outcomes. How could I create the same thing day after day? More importantly, I didn't need someone to take care of me, because I wanted to take care of myself. Through a given set of circumstances, you are where you are. What you do from now on is only up to you. It's time to change the inevitable outcomes. Through changing, we are accepting responsibility. We are thereby committing ourselves to our best potential. It is as though our innermost soul knows what is best for us but we ignore it. After having tried all alternatives to get you to listen, suddenly, the soul pipes up and tries to get your attention through people and coincidences, then through relationships and friends and finally creating the crises that are going to shake your core. When you wake up from a dream with chaos and disaster surrounding you and wonder to yourself what the hell happened to your life, you will realize that *you* are what happened to your life. You didn't listen to the warning bells in our ever-expanding world of consciousness when we do, at times, regress into pure matter of humanity. We go in search of pleasure and pain simultaneously. It is no wonder so many of us struggle for orgasm when all we respond to is pain. Nothing seems to feel right anymore, and the endless pressure is on our partners to provide us with the stimuli of desire. This, in turn, sends us into seeking a deeper and more meaningful experience, which often compels us to get hurt in some way or another, so that we can feel alive again. Our energy cells are empty because we are facing a global shortage of the only thing that can help us.

When it comes to our beliefs and judgments, we all subscribe to the crazy absolute of the following:

We are all around seven years old when we reach the age of reason. So now, packed and ready for our first day, lunchbox in hand and stomach filled with anxiety and expectation, we are exposed to order. Grand order. Everything fits into everything. Our classmates, our teachers, their superiors, our lessons, and the hierarchy of learning that pre-dates the Greeks. We are now on the knowledge train that carries historical failures in boxcars, and expectation as its engine. During a few short weeks, we discover the most fundamental part of why we are here—to learn and to base our learning on a system that pits us against what we should know and those who share our learning experiences. It is the examination or the test that will define our skills and hopefully allow us to move onto a different, perhaps higher level. The world respects knowledge through learning and the application of that into daily life in tried and tested means.

Do we let John or Mary, our buddy, our pal read all the books, make notes in case we want to check them later for review and write the tests needed until we actually have to show up for the finals?

Ahem. Ludicrous?

Headline news at seven: We all do it with our spirituality.

I have to ask those of us who are fundamental Christians ... have you read the whole Bible? To those others of us who are Jewish ... have you read the whole Torah? I can go on. The possibility exists therefore, the "what if," that you have left what you base your entire spiritual religious and creative life, to John or Mary passing your entire knowledge exam for you, without your participation, and you have just been required to show up for the occasional test. You have the notes, the cheat sheets of your religion, and you know the principal is around, because you see the structure but you don't know him or her. At all.

The love we seek has been so twisted; it has the appearance of sex and commitment in varying permutations, depending on our level of scarring. Harvesting energy and trying to grow, we are forced into corners we don't like or appreciate. We may have to come to a time in our lives where we finally understand the concept of self-realization and find that people are exactly what they create. We are what we create and our world mirrors our intentions. Those of us who seek the pleasure-pain principle of matter-humanity are only seeing the diversions in the road and not the road itself. We are being tripped by pebbles climbing up a mountain. It is as though we bury our mistakes in a hole and walk away from them, only to find that the holes now look like Swiss cheese and that cheese is our psyche. As humans, we tend to discriminate most ineffectively with ourselves—we label everything within our personalities, mind, emotions, and our spirits. If you honestly looked within your Swiss cheese pantry, how many labels are really there? Do you have them color-coded so that you can bring the red ones out when required, the blue ones for rainy days, and the green ones when days look better?

Sure, we all experience lessons in this life, and each person has his or her own unique lessons to learn; we must learn that we cannot apply a blanket principle to the human experience when it comes to the "pain" that humans feel. This just gives us all an excuse not to grow and not to change.

Why seek out the joy of love when we can just accept that it brings pain? Why seek pleasure when disappointment will only follow in its footsteps? Hey, why not sit in a heap of bullshit and lament the futility of your life and shake your fist at a God you're not convinced exists and ponder why, in self-pity from the ego, you were created in the first place? This is the easy route, my friends. It is the road you choose *after* you have shaken your fist at God and gotten an answer! Stop seeking labels, divisions, and boundaries within yourself, and stop shouting your heart down. You alone know the answers to your life. Yes, you.

Forget the past doctrines that have programmed you into an auto-human. Stop thinking that love is imperfect, that you are imperfect. You are a perfect human being created with grace and power and the control to create your own universe. Take time to explore the beauty, like an uncharted island, pretending that you are your own survivor and carry with you your own special treasure of uniqueness. Take the map that is imprinted in your DNA, and leave the pat clichés behind. For these little "words of wisdom," as they were once called, are there to block creative thought and unique individual development in the way our minds are designed to work. We always chuckle when we hear you muse about "the brain is only using one-tenth of its potential" and follow that with, "Oh well, that is life."

If one human had the creative thought to think that phrase is us, then surely 10 billion people have the sense to find another phrase to fit another unique situation. As humans, we are so conditioned that it is almost a joyous cause for mourning. If you have more than one marriage, then there is "something wrong with you." Multiple sexual partners, then you are "dirty" and you need be "stayed away from." Of course, this precludes those of us who have already self-diagnosed ourselves as "dirty" and allowed ourselves to become polluted with sexual dis-eases. There have been laws made against us, entire clothing lines designed for us, songs made especially for us. Heck, we even go so far that we walk around with these judgments of ourselves and wear them as body armor.

Pollution is the perfect term for the diseased body, for it is as though the mind has thrown away all its garbage into the body, unchecked and not recycled. Is there any wonder that the body is a polluted mass of chronic aches and pains? We do not "will" healthy bodies, any more than we accept that we own and inhabit a beautifully functioning, self-generating mass of cells that move about our DNA strands in perfect order and harmony. We need to stop polluting our environment with our waste, the junk that the mind creates—worry, stress, and dysfunction. These are the crimes of our century because it is within the human body that we see the mirror of our planet Earth. This is the lament that comes from within us: "I'm not good enough."

The wailing of undeserving propels itself into the atmosphere for everyone to absorb another day. Will you or I take upon ourselves responsibility for the hole in the ozone layer? How can we learn to love ourselves when we are so hurt? Forget about the guy next door. We have already proven with our catastrophic behavior that we can't do that. In fact, we have regressed in the love-thy-neighbor realm to such a point that we don't even know who he is.

We need to put a stop to the self-righteous idealism, because fooling ourselves is not a game we wish to play anymore, trust me. Transparent ignorance is too thin in this world now not to recognize twisting and contorting of religious values to suit our needs, and the feeding of our egos is not working for us any longer either.

You are what you are now, and it is time. The universe is calling to you to wake up and look at who you are and what you are doing with your life. The old ways are proving unsuccessful and have only distanced us more than they have brought us together. Men and women cannot look one another in the eye anymore. Children are abused and living on the streets, and layers are being peeled back from every aspect of life to expose hidden secrets. Where are you in all this? Do you pretend that this is all "the way it should be" and condone life in its entirety by your reluctance to look within and accept responsibility for your thoughts and your actions in this world?

Do you wonder why there are so many angry people in the world who walk around with angry thoughts, no loving acceptance of another human's failings; then wonder why the world is against you? You are against you, dear friend. You are the hardest on yourself, and your self-loathing has no room to accept other failings, because you want to accept that you too are not perfect. Ergo, no one else is.

It is the adolescent about to become an adult who craves fame, honor, fortune, perfection, and recognition that starts to spiral outward. When the mind-emotion-matter finally decides to look within, it is then that the soul-spirit enters with love and acceptance of the human in its incarnated form. We first learn to love ourselves in the true grace of spirit, recognizing that we are infinite beings having a finite experience. We then start to see that all other humans are having the same experience and we begin to feel compassion. This is only really achieved after we have struggled and won against the ego's drive. We have, through this experience, been bashed about and have now accumulated a significant amount of scars, wounds, and scrapes to prove that the battle has been a fierce one. Let's just say that this is the battle with the archaic form of the devil. To think that there is some self-manifested being with horns and a red tail running around corrupting innocent humans is entirely ridiculous but plausible. My view is that if you do not really believe that your God is omnipotent and omnipresent and eternal, then you must believe that there is a "bad guy" out there "challenging" a perfect, loving, and infinitely benevolent divine presence to a duel for 6 billion-plus human souls. Yes, there is good and evil. Yes, divinity inspires us to emulate itself in creation, while negativity incites us to destroy that which we have created. We all know the difference between right and wrong. You may disagree with that statement by asking, "Why do these bad things happen in this world?"

This is the first step in denying that other people are not faced with the same choices as you, and that they are indeed, by the absolute judgment, lesser mortals than you. You know the difference but they don't, and therefore they need to be taught and punished accordingly. The black-and-white of life needs to push the 256 intensities of grey as far as it can into either end of infinity.

Anyhow, it is through this process that the "letting go" begins. The ego begins to have less of a voice and the emotion-spirit. It learns to speak louder and leads us out into our "Promised Land." The land that is rich with milk and honey, rich with love and compassion for all life—everywhere! Destruction begets perfection through creation. If you honestly believe and live as though you are a perfect creation, then you will live perfect creation, for it is in love that perfection exists. There is no other secret to life. Love is everything you need to know. In love, truth is absolute. Duality cannot exist in truth, and perfection cannot accept anything other than itself. We surround ourselves with the reality of imperfection each day, because that is how we have interpreted ourselves. We are here to learn. To learn. Simple. We cannot be more perfect than we are right now—if there was a possibility of non-existence at this moment, we would be and are perfect creations. To create our lives and live as perfect creations is our lesson at this time.

No matter what your spiritual beliefs are at the time of reading, I would like you to explore the realm in your mind, the magnificence that is you. If you don't believe that some force created you, then take a moment to imagine what possibilities came into play to birth you into the human-matter of existence in this reality. For those of us who believe in a Divine Creator or Great Spirit, if we can fix on an idea of what that may represent to us.

Sit somewhere you are comfortable and maybe won't be disturbed.

Now, I would like you to focus on your body. Take a quiet moment to relax your mind. Get it out of the picture—give it something to do—like dinner or a hot bath or your happy place—just get it out of the way for this exercise. Picture your body as a thermal scan and see the areas of hot and cold, the fully functioning electric system that moves the heat around your body to maintain the temperature you need to survive. Now, move beneath this to the nerve systems and the fully functioning neurological pathways within your body. Boom! Fire! Send, receive. Thousands of impulses a second. Now, look at the veins and arteries that move blood to and from your heart to your skin and back. Wonderful. As you are musing at these perfectly firing systems that you inhabit, ask yourself the question, "What is it that strikes me the most?"

Pause here for a second to write down all the feelings you feel when you see this system working as it does. Perfect? Automatic? It happens every day without you having to plan, have a meeting with your veins and arteries, or have a boardroom seminar with your synaptic processes. You are not stressed about this, are you? Funny, that; a billion automatic processes that you cannot control, that happen without your knowledge and without your permission. The mind, including the conscious, subconscious, and super-conscious, is also working away, creating all sorts of things you are not present with. Yet, you and your cognizant mind only concern yourselves with about fifty processes that occur around you. Those are the ones you worry about, fret about, and try to control as if you are not even paying attention to the perfection that occurs within you each nanosecond of your life in this moment.

This perfection that occurs within you occurred at your origin, the moment that your spark entered your spirit. Born in entire perfection and striving for nothing other than lessons learned in compassion and love, we tend to search for that magic formula that will create our perfect world. That one moment that defines and validates all other struggles that we deem as peace and harmony with the outside world, and we are happy. It is for the Olympiad that finally, after ten years of training and coaching, meets the podium on which the gold medal of achievement is placed.

This is no more prevalent than in our expectations with children, whether they come from us or we come into contact with them as teachers, family, or friends. We project our denials, desires, and unfulfilled wishes onto these fully developed souls—with their own blueprints—in an effort to re-create our vision of perfection in our minds, transposing them on the unique personality that has come to, or through us, to help form. Children are not fully developed as human beings when they come to us, and it is indeed up to us to nourish and nurture these individuals into their full potential. We do tend to allow our own egos to dominate when we proudly view the gurgling infant as "our own," and the infant then demonstrates specific characteristics, emulating the behavior they see around them. Starting at the nursing stage, it is startling to watch an infant seek the approval of the environment around it. It knows that smiling brings on a good reaction, and crying or expressing discomfort doesn't. All that the child knows at this point is that it is loved and cared for.

Sadly, it doesn't take this newly formed human long before the programming starts to fail. We, as parents, look at the child's development in either a balanced way see this as "growing up" or in a less balanced sense, as being unloving, unappreciative, and "strange."

"Black sheep of the family."

OK, maybe they were referring to me at the time, but that label will probably stick with some of us for as long as our time on Earth allows. That judgment existed when I was two, and no matter who or what I have become, it still is in the best interest of my family to keep me in the shepherd's flock. If I do ever wind up being moved from the pen where other black sheep of the world dwell, it may require other people in my family unit to look at their lives intensively instead of comparing their lives to mine. Feet up.

"Hell, I'm going through hell! But at least I am not like my sister. I must be all right."

How many of us can recall someone in our past saying: "For God's sake, just don't turn out like your father!"

The cycle of fulfillment becomes a self-fulfilling prophesy, either for or against you. You either embrace becoming just like your father or mother, or you run so far away, you forget where home is. The acceptance of being part of the parent never becomes a realization, and all you ever do is move away from a judgment, in a spiral or a vortex. You choose the outcome. You choose the path. Just remember that at each end of the curve, there is a choice, and that is the spiral that will take you out further or bring you back where you can still make a choice to be different.

It never fails to puzzle me how a parent and a child can both view their roles in a family as being non-separate. Can a thumb decide to leave a hand?

We are all products of the specific genetic codes that, in turn, will help us achieve a unique expression of our divine spirit in this world. What we are *not* is a grand reproduction and modified edition of our parents, complete with their will and desires and their expectations for our lives. There are some of us, though, who use this formula to manipulate and deceive our parents into whatever willful gain we desire. Some of us find our own definition of unconditional love that birthing a child brings. Others, harboring a manipulative streak, find an easy target. The same can be said for parents who have at whatever point decided that their children deserve—generally in co-operation with our old friends guilt and fear—to be punished with emotional games where the child's life is free to be sacrificed at will. This will continue at the parent's discretion, metering out abuse until there is nothing left to play with and the game ends. Some parents, ill as they are, suck the life from a child and will only stop at death until they feel the love they don't have. This death can be literal, but I have witnessed children walk around this Earth whose bodies are breathing coffins. People can starve you of the nourishment you need until you are an empty shell. This is the kind of power we have.

The game is up, boys and girls. The time for conniving and hidden darkness is over. The more that love and compassion enters the world, the sooner we can abolish lies and deceit within ourselves and those around us. I know some of you out there are not capable of love at this time, but that doesn't deter the rest of us who have hope and the power to change. One step at a time. Come hell or high water, we are all going to pull together in this one.

A human chain of love is formed by linking one, and only one, hand at a time. It is with this chain that we pull out others who are stuck in the mud, trying to throw themselves off precipices in life, that we are able to amass the force required to move everyone. It is through moving yourself off the path of destruction, where your hands are grappling to keep you on the mountain of life so that you can be free to help another. You can be anything you want. All you have to believe is that you have a choice right now. You can stay as you are and believe in that perfection which will have an immediate effect on you. You can accept that change within you, and let go of all the judgments of those around you so that they may be free to pursue their own growth, unhindered by your denials. Either way, you need to free yourself to climb higher than where you are sitting at this time. Forget why you can't. Remember why you can.

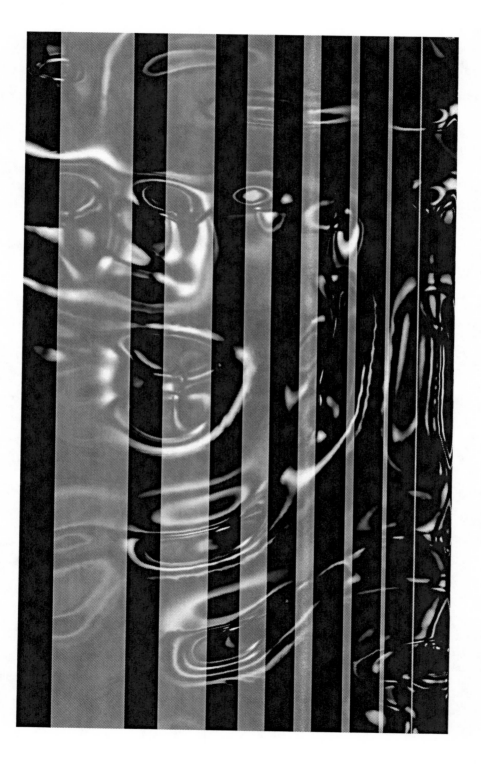

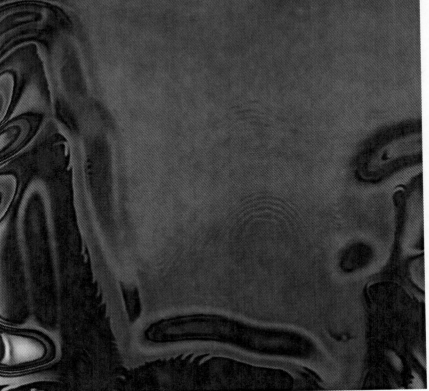

WE have been asked through many avenues to process and develop a new awareness to our environment and the lives we affect in our daily drudgery. In doing so, we have also been exposed to another phenomenon not previously accessed in our ancestral lineage: the voyage of self-discovery. My parents' generation was exposed to the falsehood of this practice, how it was seen to be selfish and self-centered to want things that were for the self, or seen in the self's best interest. It was virtually unheard of to want to live a life alone and focus on your own goals and not that of family, community, and social order. Thank heavens things are changing. These changes are being brought about by people like you and me, who are furthering our self-knowledge, getting to know who we are and why we do the things we do in our effort not only to live on this beautiful planet, but in seeing how we affect the whole. At the base of this all, we are ultimately choosing the goals of the only person who really makes us different, ourselves. If you cannot accept this role and take responsibility for your actions and who you are to yourself and your outside world, then how can you function as a whole person in your world?

Some people who have practiced this art and made specific inroads in shaping passion and creating wildly outrageous things have been, quite simply, erased. The long-term effect of this has scared the rest of us into corners that we daren't venture out of in case we are made an example of.

This has had disastrous results in our societal fabric because now we are facing depression, suicides, homicides, rapes, mass wars, and terrorism on a worldwide scale at an alarmingly increasing rate. You may tell us all that it is our deepest evil tendencies that are doing this to the world—or even worse—expand that to one person responsible for this mess.

119

Where is our responsibility in this drama? What are our choices? Is God really going to get us "in the end" if we don't fight evil? We can't win, can we? Poor, helpless, self-pitying creatures that we are. We don't have any power—nope, that is reserved for the devil that haunts us and the God that taunts us, and we are threatened in both cases with the inevitable destruction of our souls, according to a book that we never study and is never really explained to us. We can read passages. We can have blind faith that all of the holy books accurately depict how things happened back then. Who among us actually knows? Where is the absolute truth? Who is going to save us? We turn to one another, looking for facts. Proof. Fiction. Anything to help us make sense of things, which for some reason or another really don't make sense—at all. In a world where the commonest of senses is a lost art, sold for a mere pittance for convenience and routine, we all long for our "light-bulb" moment, and until then we tread the path to our deaths. This is the only place where we may get some answers eventually, so looking for something that doesn't seem to exist doesn't really matter. Some of us give up on the struggle for truth and turn to drugs and alcohol to numb the thousands of thoughts that cry out every day, wondering how a perfect world went wrong. Others turn to violence to manifest their own will to control life where people in turn have told them there is none. Dereliction. Why?

One simple answer: We gave up our authentic power to search for the sword of our youth. Our Excalibur. The one sword of truth that by pulling it out of the heart of ignorance, hate and guilt would at last make sense of everything. We would rule our world with honor and trust, and build a mighty Camelot for legends to be told of in the future. We would fight the beasts of the air that attack our positive thoughts and save innocence before it is eaten by wild beasts of abuse and neglect.

Let's propose the following scenario if you believe in none of this: In your world, the devil doesn't exist and neither does God; you don't believe in dead people, things with wings, spooks and just about everything you can't see, taste, or touch, a *Three Senses Principle*.

"If I can't actually physically perceive something, it doesn't exist."

I'll give you that a lot of people hear and smell things they pass off. Let's leave it to the three fundamental senses, then. This must make you then the creator of your world. Your school is that of tough love, hard thought, provability, and fundamental logic. You can explain how microwaves cook food when the rest of us can't *actually see* the heat. You can explain how we can talk on little plastic and metal objects through holes, to people on another continent, with wireless connections. Hell, you could even explain how we can see the skeletal structure of a human body through its clothes and see what's wrong in there. But, after all, we still need to prove in our world right now that spirit is alive and well and functioning, because unless we touch it or see it, it isn't there.

What we all can do with research is explain processes. We can predict logical outcomes based on results witnessed before, in the limited time we have taken to study the effects. The scientific masters of our time have laid many things out for us, which in the past have been too difficult to quantify because we have had the inadequate understanding to apply those theories into standard practices. Scientists and explorers all over the world struggle with a simple idiom every day: "What if?"

If it weren't for those simple two words, nothing would change.

Before you blindly label yourself as being a "this or that," stop burning to death in the fire of your pain; stop, drop, and roll. Stop and think. Drop down to the basics and roll out the books that explain it all to you. This doesn't only pertain to your spiritual belief system that is blocking truth from entering. It is also there in how you view yourself in the world. It's time to rescue yourself from the fire of hell. The pain and the smoke are becoming too much and you can't see your way clear anymore.

Stand strong in what you believe in. Never mind about the guy next door, the gossipmongers in your office, or the prostitute down the road. You fix your garden first and then let the smell of the blossoms waft down the street. A small word of advice: Judgment of any kind is bad medicine. We can watch it on TV and mistake it for retribution, but don't get caught in the emotion. Once you start looking at your belief system and what makes you as a spiritual person tick, and it's working, you should start seeing the signs of the deeds, feeling benevolent and compassionate towards all human life. If you are still on the soapbox of morality, then you are going to be clanging around your neighborhood, and the people you could really help will hear you coming a mile away and run for their lives. Above your head, flashing in Las Vegas neon, is written, "I'm OK, I know the truth and you don't."

If Jesus only knew what he was saying when he uttered, "I am the way, the truth and the life. No one can come to the Father except through me."

That passage in the Bible is so misused that plenty more people have been chased out of church seats through preconceived judgments than sit in it now. This spawned 2,000 years of prejudice and maliciousness towards others from well-meaning individuals who believed that they had the key to salvation and that no one on the planet who disagreed with them would go to heaven.

Modern scholars are looking at this "truth" in different ways with very different results. If the world is a matrix of illusion, then what are we doing here? By that I ask, *what* are we doing here? Same question we're all tired of trying to answer. The *"what"* implies responsibility. Not the fact that you were maimed, disfigured, and tortured or brutally murdered in a past life and now have a reason to preserve anger and hostility as the only expression to your pain. Pain is our commonality. We all have it and we all experience it in varying degrees throughout our life. If the sands of time were measured out in little cups, we all got the same amount. What gives one person the right to act out anger, inflict pain, and build fear in another, as opposed to responding in compassion, love, and respect? It is often more accepted to gossip and slander than it is to speak truth. Truth has been seen to be boring or harshly unapproachable. For callings as ministers and missionaries to dark countries—this is not for us, we cry. We prefer to place insecurity, doubt, and fear in someone's head, rather than respect their choice in life and love them for it, honoring their path.

"Pull them down! Tear them apart! String them from the yardarm. Tell them that they are not wanted or needed around here."

"Feed 'em to the lions."

Each one of us faces issues of choice every day, and with that comes the gift of courage and decision-making. How many times have I heard someone say that about a friend who has been physically abused in a relationship, who left and is in a safe house, only to have her actions placed in the "I know her, she'll probably go back to him" box. A response like that is a stoplight to your own fears regarding courage and limitation. Perhaps this friend of yours is in your life to show you that despite immense difficulties of control, fear, and anger, she is able to leave that life behind and try to begin a new one where she looks after herself. This situation can be even more disturbing when the abused woman begins a new relationship after a healing period and the first comment over the coffee table is, "This won't last long" or "She has a pattern of picking men who abuse her." God forbid the woman decides to go back to the situation where she feels wanted, abusive as it is. The rest of us sit in judgment like Romans in a dustbowl waiting for the next fight. There is no compassion for how she actually feels or what her real circumstances are. There is just the plain old tired, "I knew that would happen. She's so weak."

The things we do to one another. This is the result of a society that is out of control. With that I mean that they cannot control their thoughts and emotions and wind up firing the whole round of bullets into the air when the going gets tough. Bam bam! Shoot you dead before you have the chance to breathe. There is, of course, the purely vindictive societal streak that when you are in the bad box, no one wants you out because where will the Romans find their next sport if they can't throw you to the lions and watch en masse as you get ripped to shreds? This streak takes on the form that if you dare start breathing, they will shoot you until they bury you in the box, because that, according to them, is where you should stay.

The most exquisite right we have as humans is that of choice. We can choose to change ourselves and our lives and the world around us.

To walk in our own truth and see the result of living responsibly and what growth that produces if only for ourselves is worth the risk of choice. We are all going to get shot at for a time, whether we stand still or we move. Aren't we used to the holes that the emptiness is? Make a break for the border of freedom in your life, for we live in a vast ocean of people, and if it were but one teeny drop of change, creating a ripple, eventually it will create a tidal wave on the shore of time, describing the *"Butterfly Effect"*.

Change affects all of us, whether we are conscious of the change or not. We are guilty of spreading a human dis-ease that affects one another's lives without knowing how or why. Most people don't care. It's too much responsibility to worry if your actions are creating reactions in others when your own life is in turmoil. Insecure selfishness creeps in and we can wave the banner that reads "who cares" and back that up by adding the self-justification line, "They don't care about me, so why should I care about them?"

It is in the tightness of the spiral of life that we find the eternal dance of grace and joy. It is there where we accept responsibility for our lives and the effect that our lives and our actions have on those around us.

How do we bring ourselves to that point in life where we can find peace amid our own changes and that of the spirals of the lives around us and include them in the ever-changing spiral-dance of life that is creation? When do we accept that we are co-creators of our world and that we are capable of changing every atom of our body into perfection once we reach that state of grace?

There are no rules and no restrictions. There is no map. No easy way when you enter the uncharted territories of your soul of which you and you alone are the captain. You are the master of your destiny, and for the rest of us who pray and meditate and chant for the opportunity to explore our destinies, we will sit and wait for the moment that feels right enough to follow you. The only person you require for the process is the person staring at you when you look in the mirror.

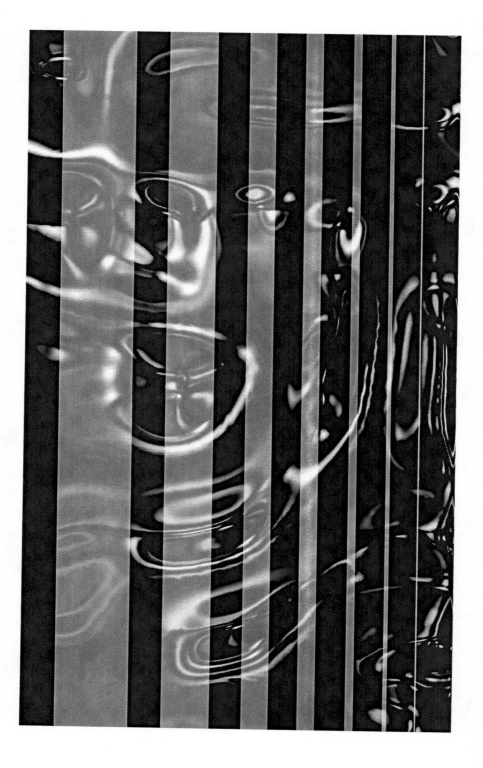

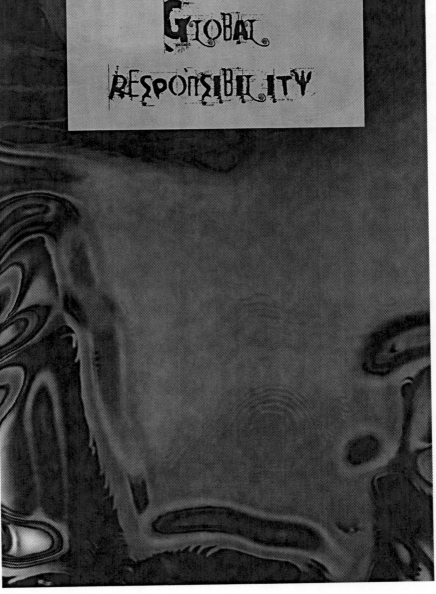

GLOBAL
RESPONSIBILITY

I HAVE so many friends who have traveled around the world and they are, by modern standards, well-versed in the global language of travel. I met someone once who described himself as a "citizen of the world." My first reaction was, "Wow! This is pretty neat, because the world is a big place."

To which he replied, "Not when you have seen as much as I have."

I admire the man, firstly for his adventurous spirit and his thirst for challenge, and secondly, for the brazen presumption that the world would actually require a citizen—albeit a self-proclaimed one. I have heard all sorts of self-proclamations on behalf of the globetrotters— from if we didn't create and now support tourism, what *would these people do for money—we had to do it,* to the quintessential commitment escape route, "Honey, you know I can't settle down until I have sailed around the world; I just wouldn't be *complete.*"

Travel entitles people to bragging rights. You seem more worldly and experienced if you have been "all over the world." I have had more than a thousand flights to date and the only thing it has exposed me to is more radiation than working in an X-ray lab, other people's problems that I can't figure out because we don't speak the same language, and a sincere appreciation for my home, family, and friends. Being an expatriate from one country, living in another and a having family on an island allows me to speak of three "homes" but leaves me equally mystified as to where I belong in the "Global Village of Confusion." It is only when I enter the silence that I find where I truly am. There, I don't have to deal with a "Revenging Montezuma," an unearthed "God of War," or whether or not the snake that just bit me will kill me in fifteen seconds; I can just stay focused on my piece of heaven. It's a simple thing, really.

In my little center of my universe, there are no screaming witches with stakes to gouge my eyes out. No warriors battling over territory, or God forbid, fighting over my lost virginity. This may be a very narrow-minded view of the world on Earth, and in such, there are beautiful things to see and do. We cannot explore beyond our borders without remaining focused on the reason for travel, to experience the self as an outer reflection, and respecting the inhabitants doing that very thing for themselves.

The inner self who is not quite in touch with itself is going to cause you much heartache and possibly even expose your tired body to extreme danger when you are traveling. Trust me. You are going to see and experience exactly what you have been putting out at home. You are now without the understanding love and compassion from poor Bob down the street, who really can't stand the fact you leave your garbage out overnight so that the crows can decorate the road with discards from your life. He, at least, understands that you are a busy person with a job you use as an excuse to escape the loveless marriage and strangulation you feel when the month-end's bills arrive, and that you are in love with your golf pro and don't have enough willpower to do anything about the situation. So, your suitcases are packed. In one of the compartments is hidden emotional baggage stowing away with you, on your journey. You think you are prepared and ready for adventure on the open road. You may be prepared with a passport with an outdated photo of yourself, travel guide, and some tips from fellow travelers on where to find clean water that won't require an emergency evacuation. This terrifies you into thinking that you are overworked but really need the holiday—where you can rest, relax, and take in the culture of your destination and forget everything. You tell yourself that you are getting away from the frustration, and the fear of the unknown manifests itself as excitement. Maybe you are alone, and the prospect of finding an exotic partner for a period of romantic time is a real possibility. After all, there are others in the world pursuing the same thing you are. Like meets like in the realm of the mind, and brings with it a magnetic force into attracting exactly what you seek. You are now a dynamic time bomb of hopes and fears, more alive that you are in your routine because every process in your body is going to be tested by traveling.

We tend to forget that all the things that we are ignoring in our lives will be worse when we return home because we have temporarily escaped the insanity. Our innate inability to change our circumstances is now front and center and we are backpacking, horse-packing, and squeezing it all in an emergency medical kit away with us. At the same time, we fool ourselves about being "globally informed" and educated, and we are the merry traveler, fully loaded with varying degrees of misinformation like the sunburns on our noses. Off we go, bringing along all the things that poison us at home; dressed in an oversized pith helmet, legs too short for the long grasses of exploration, armed with a pop gun of ignorance, trying to track down the elephant of experience.

In this state, we do not absorb anything of the places we go, the spirit or the people who can actually teach us or reflect something where we need to change. If we function from an ego perspective, we travel with the attitude of self-preservation, and in that behavior, we are arrogant and self-absorbed. We do not view our hosts as being smarter or better inclined to cope with things than we are, especially if they live in circumstances which we deem to be more primitive than what we are used to. This human ego and arrogance comparison is nowhere more visible than in the attitude of travelers not on their own turf.

You will come back with gazillions of images that you can show to Bob down the road while you sip on exotic beer brought back from the "neverlands" and fool him for a while into thinking that you are now an enlightened being on matters of a *tribal nature*. How not to eat ice, how to stay warm at minus sixty, what to take for altitude sickness, and how to dive upside down without throwing up oatmeal into your only source of air at twenty meters below the surface of a choppy sea. You are now your own *specialist* on these matters, and your experience will override any understanding that someone else has on the same subject, because you have set the authoritative criteria. No matter how old you are when someone recounts a similar tale, you will revert back to your experience, good or bad. You will, through that familiarity, paint every other picture that resembles it with the same color.

There are some of us who absolutely will not change anything about us or our lives, so the exertion of power gained through the window of a plane is used against those who are seen to be less fortunate. This power struggle goes deeper than exertion of control at home. It has been the basic motivation of exploitation and overpowering of nations, islands, countries, and their indigenous peoples. From governmental systems to food, health, sex, and religion, our historical travelers and *citizens of the world* have succeeded in polluting just about every natural habitat across our globe in biblical proportions. This doesn't only apply to our planet but the race into space with rocket ships fueled with the idiocy that we are the only ones around at this end of the universe, when we don't even have a clue on how big it actually is. Our modern-day tourist is a benign influence, dangerous nonetheless for socioeconomic reasons. It pales in comparison under their flag which the alliance of nations flies, saying, "There is no one better than us."

Could we quantify this to global arrogance? We pit our strongest against one another in sports, reveling in our victories and punishing the losers. We forget the legends of the past when they age or become too weak to fight for the country we believe in. We subscribe to the old saying that "only the strong survive", without looking at the fact that it is the strong who function by might, who overpower the meek like a giant virus absorbing everything in its path. We can't accept that another race of people is actually quite happy without us or the things we produce.

There has to be something wrong with them if they don't want what we have. How can they live without it? We will find a way to coerce them into taking what we have, because that validates our culture and everything we embrace about it. Non-believers in the ways of our world are heathens, sloths, pagans, and savages. They have to be enlightened! Being in touch with one another and the world around them is the old way, and nothing old is good. Where we live, we discard the old and treasure the new. We throw the frail into care, we lock the unstable in white rooms, we sedate our children, we tranquilize our women, we discard our professors when they start to resemble madmen, and we jail and discredit leaders who once led us to freedom from oppression. We are masters of a sterilized environment that idolizes youth and beauty. Everything else is seen as treachery. Traitors to the crown of glory will be put to death, because that is all we believe in, and aging is inevitable. It's too much bloody trouble to choose life when all it brings is more hardship.

We can't change things at home, because we feel too powerless, so we forge forth into the world and find some unsuspecting group of people whom we overpower with our money, judgments of being poor, fat, brown, ugly, or strange, and finally impose our ways with the simplest of statements—*"This is how I do it back home."*

"Well, Bronco, you ain't in Timbuktu no more."

We as modern man are not conquerors or conquistadors, and the people who think of themselves as hunters and gatherers need to take a good look at their own back yards, which need lots more hunting and gathering than was previously thought.

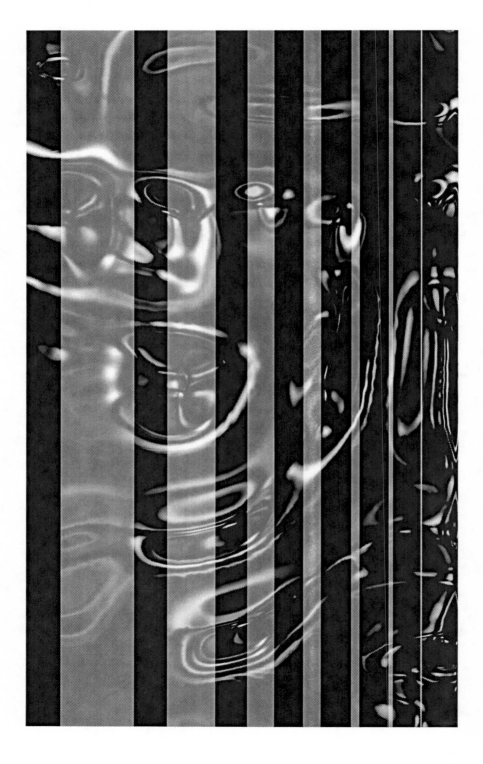

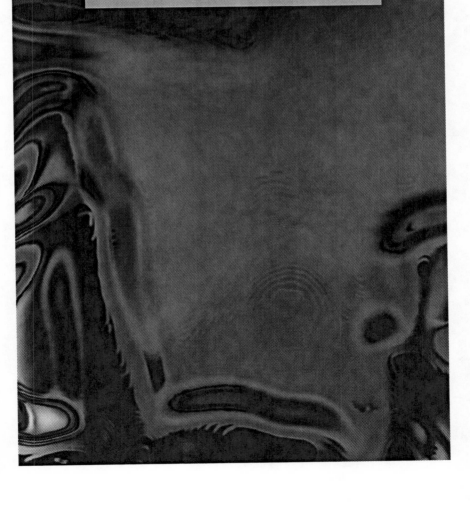

IN life, there are very few things that we perceive as abnormal. Most of those things are judged by the sight factor—what we see, what we perceive as reality. We are also conditioned to think that emotive and personal control factors are what make up our lives. We have developed our own language to deal with these factors, and tend to justify them with generalizations and blame that subtle factor called life:

"That's life, my friend!"

"Life is hard, deal with it."

"Life is what happens while you are busy making plans."

How many times have we wondered who is actually in control and how have we managed as individuals to give up the control of our extenuating circumstances. Most of us think angels, demons, spirits, guides, and signs are things that people who we perceive to be out of control need to sustain their existence. How much of reality is controllable? Is control a fascist domination of that which cannot be organized, like order out of chaos? In that theory, we are all fascists trying to dominate our environment and the people we come into contact with. We do this in our personal relationships, organizing other people's personalities and their expression of such into our own mechanisms and judging their behavior according to our own. This leads to one battle conclusion, strife. After we have judged people accordingly, we then begin to exercise punishment on them in the form of guilt. In one strangely widespread way, we all see ourselves in the reflection of God as judge and punisher. There are those people who understand that only God can judge us, and that we have to forgive those who have trespassed against us. We have to judge them first, according to our rules, before we can ascertain that they have trespassed. One needs boundaries first before they can be trespassed against, and therefore the punishing comes when we decide what to do with them after the initial trespassing has occurred.

This is an important factor to consider in our view of reality and what we do with it. What needs to be understood about reality is that it is all about judgment, whether we like it or not. Most of the judgments we have imposed are upon ourselves firstly, and this has seriously impacted our vision of what we are all capable of in life, our rules in society, and our view of everything outside of that. We have judged love—to now include specific codes and rules of conduct outside of which there is no forgiveness, only retribution. We have managed to remove any alternate potential well out of the boundaries of our judgment. People who have strayed outside the commitment of a relationship will know what I mean with this. There has been so little forgiveness that we have many types of councils to punish those who have jumped the walls of judicial systems, family politics, financial planners, and society. The strayers have found themselves in a living hell of judgment, compounded on by the guilt that has been imposed on them through their actions, and are confronted with the many faces of judgments forced on them. The only things to cling to are obsolete tools of coping mechanisms. We struggle until they we find another relationship to bring us back into the fold of normality again.

The subject of infidelity strikes fear in the heart of any person hoping for a committed relationship. We all know that the potential over the long term exists equally within the two partners, and we know that both partners at the outset will endeavor to fulfill their commitment in every cell in their body. Then suddenly, the change factor pops up—the rogue cell that mutates one day after a long day or a tedious time in trying to fit into your partner's view of what you or the relationship should look and feel like. It is an explosion within the mind that creates havoc and short-circuits everything you know to be expected of you. Suddenly, the rogue cell whispers that what you are now feeling is the right feeling, and all the anger and resentment toward your partner for snoring or ignoring or forgetting becomes a justification for this new feeling you have. The bubble of commitment becomes a cage of denied expression. The explosion occurs at a moment of your supposed weakness and the justification of an extra glass of wine or the late-night fight or a delayed flight. Suddenly, everything makes sense and the power to be something new is in your hand, and you choose the option to change your destiny forever. An implication of the power of this decision is felt the first minute after you wake up to the reality that you want everything to go back to normal. This is when you have reached the point of no return. Your partner or best friend may not be aware of this yet but you are. You know that you are now in a totally different headspace than you were a brief time ago. This is why straying spouses leave very shortly after the act of infidelity in the heat of that guilt—"Oh, God, what have I done?"

You have chosen to change your life forever. Now comes the hard part—how to deal with the new you still living in the old you's life. There is the spouse waiting for you to come home. They know something happened and it's up to them to deny their intuition or to face the change that you had the courage to bring forward. Even though victims of this situation don't like to admit it, there is never one unhappy person in a two-person relationship. One is just the catalyst, mistakenly seen as weak, but it is they who have the courage to make a change but not always having the strength to choose a more acceptable path. There may be kids, there is your job, and if your straying occurred within the confines of the workplace like 60 percent of other strayers, everything starts to hang in the balance. How do you stop the cycle from happening in the first place?

We need to look at one thing first—your view on reality. If you think that it can't be changed, you will subconsciously find a way to prove yourself wrong, because viewing reality as static in itself is wrong. Your subconscious mind is trying to tell you something that you won't hear about until you find yourself in the judgment court of something you could have been more proactive of in the first place. Going through life unconsciously is the greatest crime you can commit. It will hand you every aspect of everything you don't want to happen to your life on

Earth. Your conscious mind will fight with me here and start making up examples of all the things we know we can't change about life, like violence, terrorism, murder, and rape.

We can't look at other people and say, "Well, what about them?"

I want us to look inside and ask, "What about me?"

The terrorist is as unconscious and self-motivated as the strayer at a Christmas party. They both have internalizations and convictions and an ultimate reward for both. A terrorist inflicts fear and pain on many people he doesn't know, on behalf of the actions and convictions he has, whereas the strayer inflicts fear and pain on the people he or she loves. So, taking the subconscious theory one step further, what happens if we can tap into these areas of our brain that we think we cannot deal with and start to work with them so that the bomb doesn't start ticking at birth and go off in our faces when the people around us least expect it? I say that because each one of us knows the kind of darkness we are capable of, and we will spend most of our lives trying to cover that up, for fear that we may be discovered. This is how we turn into fascists and racists and all sorts of "-ists." We take the definitely difficult task of trying to hide our true nature without trying to find out who we really are inside, and projecting all sorts of silly ideas of control on other people.

There is no fast track from where we are right now. There are no more excuses. No lipstick messages on our mirrors. It is now up to us to change who we are. We are dis-eased. We are suffering. It's time to end the pain and embrace the only thing left to grasp: pure, unconditional love. We need to experience healing and discover our unique and authentic power grids. We are in this together, dissolving ignorance and fear one step at a time, and together we will build a world with one flawless knowledge block at a time. This perfect knowledge is that we are all beautiful, majestic creators, living without ignorance of one another, in the light, imitating the Creator of our souls and doing what we need to do. Right here, right now.

Change is your right. Take it in both hands and be in power with it. It is your destiny calling you.

ACKNOWLEDGMENTS

To the *Council of Light*. This is our testimony that the veil does not stand in the way of the Divine Plan, and that I could work through my insecurities here to be become the "I am" that is me today.

There have been quantum interactions in my life, and every single person who has lived in my time here has shaped my life. The rudeness of a banker, the distraction of a server have all functioned in unison to make me a kinder and more loving person. The monks who taught me to quieten and listen to my chaotic mind. The many authors who have given meaning to thoughts and unanswered questions and the thousands of people I have met who have instilled a quiet patience. I have loved and lost, and in that process learned more from the person than from the relationship or the breakup of it. I would also like to thank the people who have let me in to love and be loved in return. Through you, I learned to hone skills that lay dormant within me; others were cumbersome and outdated. My emotional life, for better or worse, has been heightened by all the "I love yous" I have ever meant. No less than that have been my critics and my enemies, who have taught me patience and the ability to explain myself a bit better, learning through insecurity about security and self-reliance. They have made me the person I express today, in whole or parts thereof. To my teachers, I thank you. My family for all their love and support and giving me a place to call home. My friends. Every one of you has been incredible. I thank you for sharing your life with me.

I have learned from all of you, and for that, from my soul I thank you.

September 2, 2007

Printed in the United States
94523LV00003B/352-399/A

9 781434 343956